Agriculture in depression, 1870–1940

New Studies in Economic and Social History

Edited for the Economic History Society by
Michael Sanderson
University of East Anglia, Norwich

This series, specially commissioned by the Economic History Society, provides a guide to the current interpretations of the key themes of economic and social history in which advances have recently been made or in which there has been significant debate.

In recent times economic and social history has been one of the most flourishing areas of historical study. This has mirrored the increasing relevance of the economic and social sciences both in a student's choice of career and in forming a society at large more aware of the importance of these issues in their everyday lives. Moreover specialist interests in business, agricultural and welfare history, for example, have themselves burgeoned and there has been an increased interest in the economic development of the wider world. Stimulating as these scholarly developments have been for the specialist, the rapid advance of the subject and the quantity of new publications make it difficult for the reader to gain an overview of particular topics, let alone the whole field.

New Studies in Economic and Social History is intended for students and their teachers. It is designed to introduce them to fresh topics and to enable them to keep abreast of recent writing and debates. All the books in the series are written by a recognised authority in the subject, and the arguments and issues are set out in a critical but unpartisan fashion. The aim of the series is to survey the current state of scholarship, rather than to provide a set of prepackaged conclusions.

The series has been edited since its inception in 1968 by Professors M. W. Flinn, T. C. Smout and L. A. Clarkson, and is currently edited by Dr Michael Sanderson. From 1968 it was published by Macmillan as *Studies in Economic History*, and after 1974 as *Studies in Economic and Social History*. From 1995 *New Studies in Economic and Social History* is being published on behalf of the Economic History Society by Cambridge University Press. This new series includes some of the titles previously published by Macmillan as well as new titles, and reflects the ongoing development throughout the world of this rich seam of history.

For a full list of titles in print, please see the end of the book.

Agriculture in depression, 1870–1940

Prepared for the Economic History Society by

Richard Perren
University of Aberdeen

 CAMBRIDGE
UNIVERSITY PRESS

Published by the Press Syndicate of the University of Cambridge
The Pitt Building, Trumpington Street, Cambridge CB2 1RP
40 West 20th Street, New York, NY 10011-4211, USA
10 Stamford Road, Oakleigh, Melbourne 3166, Australia

First published 1995

Printed in Great Britain at the University Press, Cambridge

A catalogue record for this book is available from the British Library

Library of Congress cataloguing in publication data applied for

ISBN 0 521 55285 0 hardback
ISBN 0 521 55768 2 paperback

CE

Contents

List of tables   *page*   vi

1 Prosperity before 1873   1
2 The great agricultural depression of 1879–1896   7
3 Gainers and losers before 1914   17
4 Temporary revival, 1914–1921   31
5 Depression of the 1920s and 1930s   37
6 Tariff protection and other assistance   52
7 The structure of rural society   62
8 Conclusion   68

Bibliography   71
Index   79

Tables

Table 1   United Kingdom home production and
imports of wheat, 1872–1913   *page* 8

Table 2   United Kingdom home production and
imports of meat, 1872–1912   8

Table 3   Wholesale prices of various agricultural
products, 1873–1913   9

Table 4   Agricultural output and shares of farm
income, 1870–1913   11

Table 5   England and Wales: value of output sold
off farms, 1914–18   35

Table 6   Agricultural output and shares of farm
income, 1920–39   46

1
Prosperity before 1873

In 1870 British agriculture was near the end of about two decades of general prosperity. At that time the predominant system was mixed farming, founded on the technical advances in crop and livestock husbandry dating back to the seventeenth century and earlier. It was a combined system where grain crops and livestock products were produced for sale but fodder crops like roots, hay, and rotation grasses had to be consumed by the livestock on the farm. They could not be sold for cash as their function was to furnish larger supplies of manure to support greater yields of cereals and also provide more fodder on which the cattle and sheep, as well as the large amounts of horse-power required to cultivate the farm, depended. Within this closed system the successful farm had to do the following: produce all that was required to return a profit to the cultivator, yield a rent to the landowner, maintain and even increase the fertility of the soil (Chambers and Mingay, 1966, *107, 133–4*). There was always a limit, imposed by climate, terrain, and managerial skills, to the output and productivity of the entirely self-sufficient farming unit. When this was reached larger yields could only be obtained by buying in extra fertilizers and feedstuffs from outside. More intensive methods were only justified if the extra expense involved was compensated for by the increased output. To make it worthwhile, purchased inputs needed to be available relatively cheaply, the gains in productivity achieved by their use relatively spectacular, and prices for output relatively high. There are signs that as this was happening in the first half of the nineteenth century, the constraints on more intensive production were progressively removed.

The modified version of mixed farming that had evolved by 1850, variously referred to as 'high farming' and 'high feeding', aimed at high output by feeding purchased oil-cake on a lavish scale, to produce increased quantities of meat and large amounts of dung. The dung, along with purchased artificial fertilizers, was lavished on the land to promote high yields of grain and fodder for the stock (Grigg, 1989, *178–9*; Jones, 1962, *104–5*; Chambers and Mingay, 1966, *ch. 7*). In the nineteenth century significant quantities of oil-cake – the crushed residue left behind after the oils used in industry were pressed from linseed, rapeseed, and cottonseed – became available. They were supplemented by imports of maize and maize-meal, clover seeds (which were planted to produce livestock feed) as well as spent grains from British town breweries. Artificial fertilizers increased in quantity and fell in price. These included bone meal, superphosphate, and nitrates, both from domestic and, more importantly, imported sources, as well as imported guano from 1835 onwards. In the early 1850s British farmers were using approximately £10 million worth of purchased inputs per annum and this had risen to £17 million by the early 1870s (Thompson, 1968, *71, 73–7*). On the demand side the rising national income and the growth of population fed the domestic market for agricultural products (Feinstein, 1972, *Table 1, 42, 55*). The growth of towns, which could now be linked to their farming hinterlands with speed and economy by rail, reinforced the value of higher output. By the 1850s the railways were penetrating Scotland, and farmers in formerly distant English counties like Norfolk and Lincolnshire were offered easy access to London. With rising living standards the urban demand for meat and dairy produce grew particularly fast and indicated to farmers what direction to follow (Chambers and Mingay, 1966, *171*).

The general prosperity of British farming before 1870 depended on the fact that the British market was still relatively untouched by foreign competitors. The repeal of the Corn Laws in 1846 had provoked fears that the country would be immediately inundated by cheap foreign foodstuffs, but this did not occur. For 30 years the repeal of the Corn Laws and the triumph of free trade brought few problems to British agriculture. Thriving trade along with gold discoveries in Australia and America helped to stimulate industrial demand and raise prices. Grain prices fell sharply from

1848 to 1850 but recovered from 1853 onwards. The Crimean War (1854–6) and the American Civil War (1861–4) interrupted cereal exports from Russia and the United States and the demand for grain from France in the disturbances of the Franco-Prussian War and Communes (1870–1) all helped to maintain grain prices (Ernle, 1912, *374–5*). British farmers also benefited from a series of mainly good harvests, although bad seasons were never entirely unknown before the mid-1870s (Chambers and Mingay, 1966, *179*). The cultivated area expanded, land values rose and land-lords increased investment in drainage and buildings. By the end of the 1860s 'high farming' had reached its peak (Tracy, 1989, *41*). In these years the only minor inconvenience from free trade was in 1865–7 when cattle plague, introduced by infected animals imported from Europe, disrupted the livestock markets. This had the effect of raising rather than lowering prices (Perren, 1970, *84– 5, 107–9*).

By 1870 the country relied on imports for about a quarter of its total cereal requirements but for only 14 per cent of its meat (Perren, 1970, *3*). Only wheat entered the country in amounts large enough to counteract the effect of growing demand on price. In the case of this cereal the country relied on imports for approximately half its needs; there was a fall in price from the high point of the mid-1850s but even wheat did not dip very far below its pre-1846 level (Chambers and Mingay, 1966, *177–8*). The general level of prices was well maintained because those of beef, lamb, butter, cheese, eggs and bacon continued to rise. The buoyancy of prices encouraged both farmers and landlords to undertake investment. For farmers this included not only the purchased feedstuffs and fertilizers referred to above, but some of those on large farms made increasing use of machinery. Threshing machines had been available since the 1830s, after 1850 more horse drills and cultivators appeared, and by 1870 it was estimated there were 40,000 reapers in use. This affected the demand for labour, especially during the peak summer period, but this was becoming more expensive anyway with migration to the towns and restrictions on the employment of children by the Gangs Act of 1867 and the Education Acts after 1870 (Chambers and Mingay, 1966, *187–90*). But not all investment was by farmers: tenants took the lead but landlords were also encouraged to undertake complementary investments. If more stock was kept and larger yields of crops obtained, then this was a reason to improve the land and enlarge the farm buildings. These items of capital expenditure were the traditional responsibility of the landlord, who took no direct part in the day-to-day business of farming. The under-draining of soils with impeded drainage was a way of ensuring a better return from expenditure on manures and cultivation. Between 1845 and 1899 about 4.5 million acres in England were drained, the major part of this work carried out before 1870 under the stimulus of high prices, mostly by large landowners in the north and west (Phillips, 1989, *242*). Although the larger and most progressive owners spent most on their estates, even the smaller and more backward estates began to modernize their buildings, fields, drains and fences in the third quarter of the nineteenth century (Mingay (ed.), 1981, 1, *233*).

The prime exemplars of high farming were the large landowners with sufficient amounts of capital to afford the sometimes lavish expenditure on their estates this type of farming required. They were encouraged to undertake it because rents were rising and such investment held the prospect of further rent increases, though it is unlikely that these investments really paid in the strict economic sense, even before 1870. A landlord who raised a tenant's rent after installing new field drains or a covered cattle yard would have obtained a higher return if he had put the money in government stock or blue chip railway shares (Thompson, 1963, *253–5*). But he was prepared to undertake agricultural investment because it improved the fabric of the estate that would be passed on to his heir as well as providing necessary reinforcement of his social position within the rural community. Before the French Revolution the leadership provided by landowners was unques-tioned, but by the mid-nineteenth century their actions for the good of agriculture were seen as a fulfilment of their duties and a justification for their position as the otherwise undeserving ben-eficiaries of an outmoded landholding system (Wilmot, 1990, *70*). Those landlords who preferred low rents and little improvement could participate in the process by leaving most of the fixed investment to the occupier. Although improvements to the fabric of the estate became the property of the landlord when the farm was vacated this did not involve loss to the tenant because landlords would give compensation for these to a departing tenant (Mingay (ed.), 1981, 1, *233*).

The heartlands of high farming and agricultural improvement were the light land, mixed farming regions of lowland Britain. These included East Anglia, Yorkshire, and the east Midlands, as well as the Lothians of Scotland. Here farms were let on annual leases and cultivated according to a strict set of rules, though these were not always strictly enforced. The sale of fodder crops off the farm was generally forbidden and there were rules about taking two 'white' crops – that is cereal crops – off the same field in successive years. These restrictions were intended to keep the land in good heart and proper crop rotations were judged to be the only way this could be achieved, but practice was modified to take advantage of local soil conditions and market opportunities (Orwin and Whetham, 1964, *118–30*). Part of the attractiveness of the system was its flexibility and ability to respond to gradual shifts in markets and to shift the balance between arable and livestock. There was no such flexibility on the western uplands where soil and climate dictated a dependence on rearing store animals being kept for future fattening in the eastern lowlands. In Wales mixed farming was only possible in fertile districts like the Vale of Clwyd and east Flintshire in the north, the valleys of the Wye, Severn and the Usk on the south-eastern border, and in the south the region running westwards from the Towy valley into Carmarthen and on into Pembrokeshire. There tenants adopted progressive methods similar to those in England, but over most of the mountainous interior of the principality farming practices remained backward throughout the nineteenth century (Howell, 1977, *ch. 8*). The sparse population of the Scottish Highlands were packed into small communities where most scratched a peasant's living on small and unimprovable crofts. From the landlord's point of view these communities had little economic value and his main source of income was the rents of large sheep farms, tenanted mainly by non-locals, that could be found in every district of the Highlands and Islands by 1860 (Mingay (ed.), 1981, 1, *88–9*). The primary function of the upland regions was not to sell direct to the urban consumer but simply to provide inputs for the lowland farmer (Whetham, 1976, *9–16*).

There was a tendency for the more enthusiastic advocates of

high farming to disregard the fact that the lavish expenditure it entailed could only be justified when prices were high. In the 25 years or so from 1846 they were kept high by a series of fortuitous circumstances shielding British farming from the full impact of foreign competition. The failure to comprehend this encouraged the complacent belief that if investment, the application of science and the principles of good husbandry were used to raise the productivity of the land they would always give farmers a sufficient cushion against foreign competition (Chambers and Mingay, 1966, *177*). If this were so there is the question of just how many farmers had this protection. The discussion of high farming has centred around what may be regarded as 'best practice', but it is not known just how general it was. Even its main publicist, James Caird, was aware he could go straight from the most advanced experimental farm in Berkshire to farmers in Surrey who used implements 'of the rudest kind' and were barely able to write their own names (Chambers and Mingay, 1969, *172*). There has been considerable debate as to just how effective these techniques, particularly underdraining, were at improving the English clays (Sturgess, 1966, 1967; Collins and Jones, 1967; Phillips, 1969). The removal of the barriers to competitive imports from 1870 onwards affected grain prices first and then livestock products after 1880. Once this shield was gone the fragility of the system and of British agricultural prosperity was revealed, and successful adjustment to the new situation required farmers to be flexible and innovative. But in addition to the problem of depression caused by foreign competition there was a second and entirely separate feature. Agriculture was declining in importance within the national economy because manufacturing and services were growing faster. This is a normal part of the process of economic growth, and British agriculture had been experiencing relative decline for at least a century before 1850 (Crafts, 1985, *38–44, 47, 132–4*). Part of the reason for the atmosphere of depression was that this relative decline had been masked to farmers by agriculture's own expansion of output and the general growth of the economy. But after 1850 most of the other important indicators of the agricultural sector, such as the size of its labour force (Taylor, 1955), and its contribution to the nation's food supply and economic welfare, underwent absolute decline (Ojala, 1952, *66–7*).

2
The great agricultural depression of 1879–1896

The initial impact of depression was felt in the late 1870s and early 1880s. At first the long-term decline in cereal prices was masked by a run of bad seasons and poor harvests from 1875, culminating in one of the wettest years on record for 1879. When the Prime Minister, Benjamin Disraeli, took a walk in one storm that year and came upon a group of his farmers he asked if 'the dove had left the ark yet'. Continued wet weather in 1880 and 1881 brought about sheep rot, causing an estimated loss of 6 million animals worth a total of £12 million (Jones, 1964, *173–4*). In previous poor seasons farmers had some compensation for low yields in the high prices brought about by shortage. By the 1870s the American Civil War (1861–5) was over, railways were extended westwards into the great corn-growing plains, steam navigation drastically reduced the price of ocean freight and Chicago developed as a great agricultural processing, storage and marketing centre. Similar kinds of developments affected the farmers and products of other countries and continents. The world grain market was eventually supplied from Russia, Asia, and both South and North America. Freezing works and refrigerated ocean transport allowed perishable foods like meat, butter, eggs and fruit to be brought to Britain from America, New Zealand and Australia (Orwin and Whetham, 1964, *240–1*; Ernle, 1912, *377–9*, Perren, 1978, *chs 7 and 10*; Harley, 1992). Their combined effect was a vast increase first in the cereals and then the meat and dairy products available on world markets between 1870 and 1914. The impact of these developments on the British wheat and meat supplies can be seen in Table 1 and Table 2. Along with the increase in supply came a large reduction in price, which is shown in Table 3. The price fall after 1870 deprived

Table 1 *United Kingdom home production and imports of wheat, 1872–1913 (million cwt)*

	1872	1882	1892	1902	1913
Home production	50.7	44.7	33.6	32.2	31.1
Imports[a]					
Europe	9.7	5.6	0.6	–	–
Russia	17.9	9.7	4.4	6.6	7.6
United States	9.6	45.0	60.9	65.0	37.2
Canada	2.2	3.1	5.8	12.2	26.5
Argentina	–	–	3.4	4.5	20.5
India	–	8.5	12.5	8.8	24.3
Australasia	0.5	3.1	2.1	4.4	11.5
Other countries	7.5	5.7	5.9	6.4	3.5
Total imports	47.4	80.7	95.6	107.9	131.1
TOTAL	98.1	125.4	130.2	140.1	162.2
Per cent imports	48.3	64.4	73.4	77.0	80.8

[a] Imports include wheat flour in grain equivalents.
Sources: Home production, Ministry of Agriculture and Fisheries, *Report of the Committee on the Stabilisation of Agricultural Prices*, 1925, Appendix I. Imports, *Annual Statements of Trade*.

Table 2 *United Kingdom home production and imports of meat, 1872–1912 (million cwt)*

	1872	1882	1892	1902	1912
Home production	26.6	25.6	28.2	29.1	29.7
Imports[a]	4.2	9.0	13.5	20.3	21.8
TOTAL	30.8	34.6	41.7	49.4	51.5
Per cent imports	13.6	26.0	32.3	41.1	42.3

[a]Includes imports of live animals slaughtered for meat in the UK.
Source: Perren, 1978, 3.

British cereal growers of their traditional compensation for poor seasons.

The decline in wheat prices began in 1873, with a temporary rise in 1876 and 1877 because of the Russo-Turkish War. In the 1860s the average official price of British wheat, as published in the *London Gazette*, was 51s. 1d. (£2 55p) per quarter but by 1879 it had declined to 43s. 10d. (£2 19p) and continued to fall through

Table 3 *Wholesale prices of various agricultural products, 1873–1913*

	1873		1880		1888		1896		1913	
Cereals[a]	*s.*	*d.*	*s.*	*d.*	*s.*	*d.*	*s.*	*d.*	*s.*	*d.*
Wheat	58	8	44	4	31	10	26	2	31	8
Barley	40	5	33	1	27	10	22	11	27	3
Oats	25	5	23	1	16	9	14	9	19	1
Livestock										
Beef[b]	5	5	4	10	4	0	3	9	4	6
Mutton[b]	5	11	5	6	1	10	4	5	5	2
Pork[b]	4	6	4	7	3	4	2	11	4	7
Bacon[c]	81	0	76	0	61	0	50	0	77	0
Wool[d]	28	7	17	8	12	1	13	5	14	5
General index[e] of food and raw material prices	111		88		70		61		85	
Index of food[e] prices	107		94		72		62		77	

[a]per quarter (c. 495 lb); [b]per 8 lb; [c]per cwt; [d]English longwool, per 14 lb; [e]1867–77=100
Source: A. Sauerbeck, 'Prices of Commodities and the Precious Metals', *Journal of the Statistical Society*, XLIX (1886) and continued annually thereafter in the same source.

the 1880s, reaching a low point of 22*s.* 10*d.* (£1 14p) in 1894 (Olson and Harris, 1959, *146–7*). Although prices of oats and barley also declined their position was not as serious as wheat. For livestock products, with the exception of wool, the price fall was less severe. Because there is no official series, livestock product prices are less easy to obtain but best English beef at London's Smithfield Market fell by 11 per cent between 1867–71 and 1894–8 (Fletcher, 1961, *419–20*; Murray, 1931, *62–3*). The decline in wheat was most serious, but at the same time it has to be remembered that the prices of all commodities fell between 1873 and 1896, so what is important is not that agricultural prices fell but whether they fell faster than prices in general, including the cost of labour. Between 1873 and 1896 average prices fell by 40 per cent, but those of meat and dairy produce fell by less than this, oats and barley declined by about the same amount as the general price level and only wool and wheat, with falls of 50 and 51 per cent, respectively, declined by more than this (Layton, 1920, *53, 88*). As money wages remained unchanged this meant that although farmers had to pay more in real terms for labour, there was also more purchasing power within the community at large (Feinstein, 1972, *Table 65*). The combination of cheap cereals and growing prosperity meant that people could easily meet their basic food requirements, leaving a larger proportion of their incomes to spend on higher quality protein foods such as meat, dairy products, fresh vegetables and fruit (Orr, 1938, *17–19*). As a result *per capita* consumption of wheat, which in 1914 accounted for over 90 per cent of British food grain consumption, was more or less stable between 1885 and 1914, and actually declined between the wars (Collins, 1993, *21, 23*).

The different behaviour of prices for cereals and animal products had important implications. Hardest hit were those corn growers in the south-east on heavy clay land for whom wheat was an important cash crop. They had problems working this land in the wet seasons, and as their labour costs were higher than light-land farmers they were particularly vulnerable to low prices. But they were only a fraction of all British farmers, and even before the depression arrived cereals were only a small part of the total value of British agricultural output. In 1870–6 wheat, barley and oats made up only 18.1 per cent of the value of UK agricultural output, and wheat alone accounted for only 8.4 per cent. By 1911–13 the share of all cereals had declined to 10.3 per cent and wheat to 4.1 per cent. We can see from Table 4 that the bulk of output in 1870–6 was livestock products with meat, milk, wool, eggs, poultry and horses making up 66 per cent and by 1911–13 they accounted for 75 per cent. The most important of these were meat at 41.8 per cent and 41.9 per cent in 1870–6 and 1911–13 and milk, which grew from 17.8 per cent to 23.8 per cent between the same dates (Ojala, 1952, *209*). This increased emphasis on livestock also saw a decline in the acreage of tillage from 45.5 per cent of the total under crops and grass in 1866–75 to 32.5 per cent in 1906–15, and a rise in the permanent grass acreage from 40.9 per cent to 54.4 per cent. The acreage of temporary grass hardly changed, a fall in England and Wales being almost counterbalanced by its increase in Scotland (MAFF, 1968, *13*). Wherever possible, British agricul-

Table 4 *Agricultural output and shares of farm income, 1870–1913*

	Gross agricultural output (£ million at 1911–13 prices)			Share of farm income (per cent)		
	Crops	Livestock	Total output	Wages	Rent	Farmers' income
1870–76	69.86	136.11	205.97	37	34	29
1877–85	63.73	136.95	200.68	42	40	18
1886–93	60.14	148.12	208.26	42	37	21
1894–1903	57.21	154.64	211.85	43	33	24
1904–10	57.54	161.63	219.17	41	31	28
1911–13	56.23	165.89	222.12	40	29	31

Sources: Output, Ojala, 1952, *209*; Income, Crafts, 1985, *Table 23*.

ture reacted to depressed grain prices by turning to the livestock sector, as can be seen in Table 4, because its prices were the most buoyant.

In his classic work, *English Farming Past and Present*, written in 1912, Lord Ernle painted a picture of prosperity starting to ebb from 1864 and then severe depression for all sections of agriculture beginning in 1874 and continuing 'throughout the rest of the reign of Queen Victoria and beyond' (Ernle, 1912, *377*). The contrast was made even more emphatic by his description of the ten years 1852–63 as a 'golden age' (ibid., *373*). Ernle's thesis of general depression was drawn from material published by the two Royal Commissions on Agricultural Depression of 1879–82 and 1894–97 (RC Reports, 1881, 1882; 1894, 1895, 1896, 1897). T. W. Fletcher has since pointed out that the membership of the first of these bodies was biased towards aristocratic landowners with estates in corn-growing districts of southern and eastern England. Out of 35 farmers selected to give evidence to the 1879–82 Royal Commission, chaired by the Duke of Richmond, 26 were tenant farmers with large cereal farms in the 'corn' counties of the east and south. Only nine came from the 'grazing' counties of the north and west, and two of these farmed in the arable East Riding of Yorkshire (Fletcher, 1961a, *425–7*). This Royal Commission and its Preliminary Report, issued in 1882, stressed the universal nature of the depression and paid little attention to the fact that livestock farmers were relatively untroubled by the fall in wheat prices (RC Report, 1882).

A second Royal Commission, appointed in 1894, under the chairmanship of G. J. Shaw-Lefevre, included a majority of commoners and more representatives of the pastoral northern and western districts (RC Report, 1894). The farmer witnesses who appeared before it still included 22 from the east and south but those from the north and west now numbered 18. The members were much more divided in their views about the nature and the severity of depression. By this time the prices of animal products had fallen, but a section of the Commission rightly believed that the depression was much more serious in the arable districts of the south and east than in the livestock-producing north and west. They made the point that drought in 1892 and 1893, which was one of the immediate reasons for appointing this Royal Commission, had greater adverse effects on corn growing than on livestock production, and that the south and east suffered most because they were the chief wheat-growing districts. In addition, large corn-growing farms had been most seriously hit by rising costs of hired labour, but small family farms, which were the preponderant type in the pastoral north and west, used comparatively little hired labour (Fletcher, 1961a, *428–9*). But even this second Royal Commission showed no common understanding of the shifts and changes in costs and prices that were occurring in the agriculture of the western world. As corn prices fell, farmers switched their emphasis to livestock products with the result that the value of national output declined from 1870 to 1896, but by 1914 had returned close to its level of 1870 (Turner, 1993, *40–4*).

One price change positively helped the livestock producer. The greater decline of cereals reduced the real cost of purchased feedstuffs and shifted the ratio of livestock to feed prices in the livestock producer's favour, making purchased feedstuffs at least 30 per cent cheaper between 1867–71 and 1894–8 (Fletcher, 1961a, *430*). Livestock farmers thus had a double incentive to expand output, namely a fall in their production costs and a continually rising demand for their products. Most of these enjoyed a greater degree of protection from the competition of imports than cereals, due to transport difficulties and the higher quality of livestock products. T. W. Fletcher estimates that the value of gross output from Lancashire livestock farms rose by a third during the Great Depression. The fall in the price of animal feed not only reduced costs but, along with a reduction in labour costs and an unchanged level of rents, it also allowed a 60 per cent increase in the amount of feed purchased (Fletcher, 1961b, *36–7*).

Although livestock farmers were by no means untouched by the major shifts in the world food supplies after 1870, they had far more options open to them than corn growers. As Britain came to rely more on cheap imported factory-made American and European cheese and butter after 1870, British dairy farmers moved into the fresh milk trade where there was no foreign competition. The railway and refrigeration together vastly expanded the hinterland from which all towns could draw milk supplies (Taylor, 1976, 1987). After a period of doldrums in the 1850s and 1860s London's demand for milk expanded after 1870, growing at around 25 per cent per decade from 1880 to 1910 (Atkins, 1977–8, *222*). In the late 1870s wholesalers began to set up cooling depots at country railway stations to receive the milk delivered by farmers. By 1879 the North Wiltshire Dairy had buildings for this purpose at Swindon, in 1881 the Surrey Farm Dairy Company had a depot at Tisbury in the same county, and the Amalgamated Dairies were building a depot near Derby. In 1860 the London 'milkshed' only extended to about 25 miles (Whetham, 1964, *374–5, 379*). By 1900 the farms best suited to supply the growing demand for railway milk were those within 100 miles or so of a city and near a mainline station, although London drew its supplies from farms as much as 200 miles away (Pratt, 1906, *8–24*; Brown, 1989, *47*). Those who specialized in meat animals did best by concentrating on high quality beef and lamb as the increasing imports of chilled and frozen meat were generally only a serious threat to lower grade domestic beef and mutton (Orwin and Whetham, 1964, *261*; Perren, 1978, *160, 166, 196–7*). This provided particular opportunities for the feeders of north-east Scotland to supply the London market with prime cuts of Aberdeen Angus beef and for Welsh lowland farmers to supply prime mutton and lamb (Perren, 1978, *146–7*; Keith, 1954, *152*; Howell, 1977, *146*).

Another area to expand after 1870 was the horticultural industry, taking advantage of an increased market for fruit and vegetables (Channing, 1897, *32, 35*). Between 1870 and 1910 the area under orchards in Great Britain increased by 84,000 acres (Robinson, 1988, *98*), whilst the acreage of small fruit rose from 54,000 in 1891 to 77,000 in 1914 (Ernle, 1912, *513–14*). The depression helped to bring about the expansion of horticulture in previously localized midlands and home counties centres, such as the Vale of Evesham and Sandy in Bedfordshire as well as stimulating interest in new areas such as Worthing, Spalding and the Isle of Axholme. The country around Wisbech in Cambridge-shire was once devoted entirely to wheat, but by 1900 a total of 15,000 tons of fruit a year was being sent by rail to all the major cities. In addition, the jam factories of Messrs Chivers at Histon near Cambridge provided another outlet for the increasing amount of fruit grown in that county. In the country as whole there were between 200 and 300 jam-makers, and the five largest used 20,000 tons of fruit (Pratt, 1906, *41–5, 51–2*). The opportunities for farmers to expand into fruit and vegetables varied. Whereas some vegetables grown as field crops, such as maincrop potatoes, brassicas, carrots and peas, could be worked into existing arable rotations it was not possible to do this with fruit (Astor and Rowntree, 1938, *124, 141, 157*). For this reason fruit growing was much more cut off from other branches of farming and was less attractive to the ex-arable farmer seeking to diversify than vegetable culture; in most cases the fruit grower was a smallholder. Although the total fruit acreage involved was small, at less than 3 per cent of all agricultural land in 1895, its importance lay in the high value output from this small area (Robinson, 1988, *100–17*).

The switch to livestock products was not an entirely new departure after 1870. Eric Jones has suggested that even during the era of high farming, farmers were already switching emphasis from cereals to livestock when rising prices for the latter meant improved profits. The long-term influx of grain from North America, and the movement of product prices in favour of livestock and at the expense of cereals had been forecast by one farming writer, James Caird, as early as 1849. In the 1850s and 1860s mixed farming systems had been retained because the disparities in the returns between livestock and cereals were not so extreme as they were to become later. Before 1870 farmers could still run the system at a profit, relying on the returns from livestock for the majority of their income and using them for additional income, feeding more to livestock in years of low grain prices. After 1870 the failure of one side of the whole system, by the collapse of grain prices, brought about the break-up of mixed farming (Jones, 1962).

But salvation was possible, even for farmers in the corn-growing districts. The Earl of Leicester abandoned four-course rotation on his Norfolk estate, laid corn land down to grass and fattened sheep for a profit. Few parts of the country were beyond the reach of a local market or the growing demand from the conurbations (Fletcher, 1961b, *27–38*). Smallholders around Heathfield in Sussex specialised in fattening poultry for the London market. In Cornwall farmers around Penzance took advantage of the demand for early season vegetables and other market garden crops. In Ayrshire some farmers specialised in dairying while others concentrated on the production of early potatoes (Hall, 1913, *47, 341–7, 393–407*). Writing in 1897, Francis Channing reported a number of instances where farmers had successfully adapted to lower prices by developing new enterprises. He even gave examples where mixed farming continued to pay, though only after rents were substantially reduced. But most of his instances of success are of farmers who relied heavily on those new lines of enterprise already referred to, such as dairying, poultry and pig fattening, market gardening and fruit. Farmers with a reputation as producers of special types of livestock, such as pedigree pigs, sheep and cattle, or good quality horses, had advantages that no fall in prices could take away (Channing, 1897, *28–35, 36*). In their case there was also a buoyant export trade with America and Europe that they could take advantage of if home demand was slack. Exports of British cattle and sheep rose from £3.1 million in 1875–9 to £13.5 million in 1895–9 (Whetham, 1976; Orwin and Whetham, 1964, *269, 270, 361*). Channing believed that successful adaptation required three things: the ability and energy of the individual farmer; a landlord who allowed him free scope of action; and, 'most indispensable of all, adequate capital' (Channing, 1897, *51*).

Yet, in spite of Fletcher's modification of Ernle's picture of general depression, the term 'great agricultural depression', or variations on it, has not been banished from the literature since the appearance of his two articles in 1961 (Fletcher, 1961a, b). In 1974 P. J. Perry titled his book *British Farming in the Great*

Depression 1870–1914 (Perry, 1974) and Chambers and Mingay also use the phrase 'the great depression' in their book, while admitting that the price fall in the last quarter of the nineteenth century was not universally disastrous (Chambers and Mingay, 1966, *181*). F. M. L. Thompson has recently suggested that part of the reason for the persistence of the term was the 'money illusion'. Although all prices, and not just those of agricultural products, were falling from 1879 to 1896 farmers felt worse off because their own money incomes were reduced, even though their purchasing power was unchanged (Thompson, 1991, *212–13*). General prices stabilised after 1896 and up to 1914, but so too did those of farm products, which meant that the money illusion did not fuel complaints just prior to the First World War. But for approximately 15 of the 45 years from 1870 to 1914 farm prices fell faster or rose less than all prices, and for farmers there was nothing illusory about the fall in their real incomes (Thompson, 1991, *214*).

3
Gainers and losers before 1914

The effects of depression on the three economic groups involved in farming were unequal. An attempt has been made by Cormac Ó Gráda to find out who gained and who lost (Ó Gráda, 1981). Information on agricultural incomes is not readily available, but he has provided an approximate guide to the average real income from agriculture for groups of years together with the percentage claimed by landlords, farmers and workers. He finds that landlords fared worst with a decline of about 30 per cent in their income from the land between 1880–2 and 1900–2, after which the decline halted. Farmers, both owners and tenants, did not do as badly, in spite of the fall in their income in the late 1880s and early 1890s, which can be seen from Table 4. However, their incomes rose by an average of 14 per cent between 1861 and 1911 (although it was only 10 per cent between 1871 and 1911). But the group who fared best, mainly because of the huge decrease in their numbers from over 1.4 million in 1861 to around a million in 1911, were farmworkers, whose average incomes rose by over 50 per cent (Ó Gráda, 1981, *176–9*; Orwin and Whetham, 1964, *342*).

For landlords, the most powerful force at work in reducing their share of income from agriculture was the decline in rents. Our information on this subject is sketchy and the rent indices we have are heavily influenced by series from estates in the corn-growing counties of eastern England. Although work is going on to produce a more geographically and agriculturally representative series, we must accept that those available at present are likely to overstate the extent of decline (Turner, 1992, *50–1*). This is because evidence from individual estates supports the thesis that rents fell more in arable eastern England than in the pastoral north and west

(Perren 1970, *39*). When pressure on cash flows increased during the depressed agricultural conditions of the later nineteenth century, the payment of rent became of the greatest concern for many tenants. In the short term their incomes fell first, as can be seen from Table 4, and their immediate response was to ask the landlord to lessen this burden in some way as paying excessively high rents, however defined, was an easily accepted explanation of agricultural difficulties (Campbell, 1991, *137*). On three estates in south-west Scotland, belonging to the Earl of Galloway, Murray-Stewart of Broughton and Cally, and Agnew of Lochnaw, rentals rose in the 1870s as farms were let out in the last years of general prosperity at levels of rent that were shortly to prove highly contentious. The Galloway rental reached its peak in 1878, the Broughton rental in 1880 and on the Lochnaw estate the peak came in 1882; by 1900 all had fallen sharply from their respective peaks with falls of 6.4 per cent for Broughton and Cally, 16 per cent for Lochnaw and 24.6 per cent for the Galloway estate (Campbell, 1991, *138*). The severity of reductions depended on both type of soil and type of farming. Guy's Hospital had estates in Essex, Lincolnshire and Hereford and it was the heavy claylands of the Essex estate that felt the earliest and most extreme rent reductions. On the Duke of Sutherland's dairying claylands around Trentham in Staffordshire reductions needed were comparatively small. In the cattle-rearing districts of eastern Shropshire where the Sutherlands had estates, and on the Guy's properties in Herefordshire, falling livestock prices in the late 1880s and early 1890s had effects similar to the earlier fall in wheat on the Essex clays (Robinson, 1988, *129–45*). Although depression in the cattle-rearing districts was less severe and shorter lived than on the Essex clays, sheep farming was somewhat more affected by declining prices. Sheep farmers in England and Wales generally managed to adapt to the changed conditions, but there were particular problems for some large Highland estates. Here reduced wool and mutton prices in the 1880s and the lack of alternative products, actually bankrupted some of the tenants, thus depriving their landlords of an income from this source and forcing them to let the land for sporting (Brown, 1989, *41–4*; Mingay (ed.), 1981, 1, *88–90*; 2, *485*).

In some instances tenants were granted temporary reductions, or allowances, to enable them to buy inputs such as bonemeal. Arrears of rent were allowed to accumulate and substantial aid was given on some estates by granting allowances for fertilizers and writing off rent arrears (Campbell, 1991, *138–40*). These strategies were often more attractive to landlords than straightforward reductions in rent because they seemed to represent no permanent loss. Ernle gives the impression that losses in the 1870s and 1880s were so great that by the 1890s neither tenants nor landlords had sufficient capital left to adapt to new conditions (Ernle, 1912, *383*). But not all landlords were prevented from assisting their tenants by lack of finance. Their ability to help depended on the total size of their resources and this could include income from other than agricultural land as well as industrial and urban residential property. There is evidence that landlords in this position, such as the Dukes of Westminster, Bedford, and Sutherland, were still prepared to continue expenditure on their agricultural properties, even though it was clearly ill-advised from a strictly economic point of view, up to at least the turn of the century (Thompson, 1963, *309–17*; Perren, 1970). Ó Gráda believes that such practices were an extreme case of throwing good money after bad, though Perren takes the view that in some instances they may at least have stemmed the fall in rents (Ó Gráda, 1979; Perren, 1979). Although regional variations were strong, it needs to be stressed that over large parts of the country there was little distress, and little need for landlords to make sacrifices or adjustments. In the regions of family farmers and livestock production, farming went on and rents were paid. On Sir Frederick Knight's Exmoor estate rents were paid in full, and the fifth Marquess of Ailesbury succeeded to a run-down practically bankrupt Wiltshire estate in 1894 but by prudent management was able to repair or rebuild the farms, and at his death in 1911 pass on an unencumbered estate to his successor (Orwin and Whetham, 1964, *313–14*). The level of landlord income was best preserved in Lancashire, Cheshire, Shropshire and Staffordshire, but for those with estates in East Anglia, Essex, Wiltshire, Oxfordshire, Berkshire or Kent rental values declined by over 36 per cent between 1873 and 1911 (Thompson, 1991, *224, 227*).

P. J. Perry has used bankruptcy rates as an indicator of depression for farmers (Perry, 1972; 1974, *26–34*). He extracted from the notices of bankruptcies in England and Wales recorded in the *London Gazette* those among farmers for 1871–3, 1881–3 and 1891–3. These data were used to produce a series of national maps showing on an individual and on a county basis just where farmer bankruptcies were located in the three groups of years. The number of bankruptcies was just over 150 in 1871–3, almost 700 in 1881–3 and just under 500 in 1891–3 (Perry, 1972, *31–3, 40*). The first thing that needs to be noted is that even though in the very worst group of years there was a five-fold rise in the number of bankruptcies over those recorded for the early 1870s, the total failures in those three years only amounted to one in 320 of the farmers in England and Wales in 1881 (Taylor, 1955, *38*). This can hardly be regarded as widespread bankruptcy, although figures of formal bankruptcy do not include individuals in difficulty who made some sort of private arrangement with their creditors. Perry's analysis also shows that the highest numbers of bankruptcies were found in the arable east of England, both in 1871–3 and in 1881–3, although there were some individual concentrations in livestock counties of the west. Perry explains these by reference to special local factors, thus he notes that the high rates for the 1880s in Cheshire, east Lancashire, and the West Riding are probably a reflection of a large number of small farmers rather than of extremely intense depression (Perry, 1972, *37*). This underlines the fact that one problem in interpreting these data is that the bankruptcy of a very small farmer has as much weight as that of a very large one. In an attempt to measure farmers' perceptions of depression, Perry shows maps comparing county levels of bank- ruptcy in the 1880s and 1890s with those of the 1870s as well as levels in the 1890s compared with those of the 1880s (Perry, 1972, *41, 43, 44*). From this he concludes that depression was more widespread in the 1890s, even though its incidence was reduced from that in the 1880s. This would be in accord with the view that livestock farmers were more affected by the fall in animal prices by the 1890s. Although F. M. L. Thompson has expressed reserva- tions about Perry's sources of data (Thompson, 1991, *22–3*), his analysis does provide a valuable corrective for any tendency to overstate the contrast between the experiences of the east and west of England.

Farmers from all regions were vocal in their complaints but, like the landlords, those who suffered most were clayland corn growers of eastern England who did not have the flexibility to switch to other enterprises. To some extent the landlord acted as a buffer between the farmer and the market and provided a cushion from the worst effects of falling prices by rent remissions and expenditure on the farms. In addition, farmers gained extra protection from the tenant right legislation of 1875 and 1883 which gave them compensation for unexhausted improvements when they quitted their farm, although in some parts of England landlords had been in the custom of paying compensation to departing tenants well before 1870 (Orwin and Whetham, 1964, *172, 247*; Grigg, 1989, *108*). Even so, not all tenants had either the inclination or the expertise to switch to completely new types of farming and an unknown number were either forced or chose to give up. In eastern England some traditionalist arable farmers appear to have viewed what they called 'cow keeping' with disdain and refused to adopt it (Fletcher, 1961a, *431*; 1961b, *38*).

Sometimes landlords would have to take run-down farms in hand and spend money on land and buildings before reletting them at lower rents. This was undesirable, but generally it was possible to find replacement tenants. At the 1871 census there were 305,000 farmers in Great Britain, this fell to 279,000 in 1881 but thereafter remained practically constant and there were 280,000 in 1911 (Orwin and Whetham, 1964, *342*). Most of the men that landlords' land agents recruited to regenerate run-down Lothians, Essex or midlands arable farms seem to have come from western Britain. Livestock farmers from Devon and Cornwall, hill farmers from Wales and the Welsh border, dairy farmers from Ayrshire, and Highland farmers, schooled in cattle keeping and milk production often with some experience in growing field crop vegetables, injected new techniques and methods of management. Not all the immigrants succeeded, but enough did, along with the more enterprising locals, to break down the old reliance on mixed farming (Orwin and Whetham, 1964, *274–7*). On the Essex clayland estates of Lord Rayleigh the farms were successfully managed by his brother the Hon. Edward Strutt. Between 1876 and 1896 the land in hand rose from 850 acres to 4300 and by 1914 he was farming nearly 6000 acres. He developed a successful system of intensive arable dairying, supplying milk to the London market and averaging a profit of 24s. an acre between 1896 and 1914 (Gavin, 1967, *81–103*). The changed circumstances required flexible systems of cropping to turn output into cash more quickly. The case was the same for livestock production, usually done by specializing in milk like Edward Strutt, or else by the rapid fattening of cattle in 12 or 18 months instead of three years.

The improvement in the fortunes of the farmworker over this period owed little to the brief burgeoning of agricultural trade unionism in the 1870s (Dunbabin, 1968). In the south-eastern counties, where unions had most members, wages were actually lower and rose more slowly than in the rest of the country (Dunbabin, 1974, *68, 238–41, 302*). The weakness of the farm-worker's position lay in the fact that, unlike the industrial worker, he was employed either singly or in small groups, which made combination less easy and, if there was any dispute over pay, it was always possible for the farmer to find a substitute. The major factor strengthening the farmworker's bargaining position after 1870 was the flight from the land. There were two possible destinations for those who left: emigration overseas and migration to the towns and cities of Britain. Together these reduced the number of all full-time farmworkers in England and Wales by 23 per cent, from 891,000 in 1871 to 688,000 in 1911. In Scotland, where the pressure to move was greater, the fall was greater and full-time farmworkers declined by 36 per cent between the same dates, from 165,000 to 106,000 (Taylor, 1955, *38, 39*).

Overseas emigration from England and Wales was 160,000 in 1871–80 and increased to over 600,000 in 1881–90, then fell back sharply in the 1890s (Armstrong, 1988, *115*). There were attempts to encourage migration from some rural areas with a large labour surplus in the 1870s. Canon Girdlestone, in the Devon parish of Halberton between 1866 and 1872, disseminated publicity about job opportunities elsewhere. His efforts resulted in the movement of 400 to 500 families, but most of these moved to other places in England (Orwin and Whetham, 1964, *222–3*). The agricultural trade unions also took part in this search for alternative employment opportunities. Late in 1873 Joseph Arch of the National Agricultural Labourers' Union was sent by the union to Canada to investigate the prospects there for the farmworker. He returned impressed and convinced by the Canadian government's assurance that any men would be looked after and settled on the land, although in the late 1870s economic problems caused many of the Dominions, including New Zealand, to phase out their assistance schemes. But the majority of emigrants were from the towns and cities and not the countryside; in the 1880s, the decade of highest emigration in the nineteenth century, only a sixth of British emigrants were agricultural workers. The chosen destination of most workers leaving the land was not overseas but the urban centres of Britain. There was a reluctance for sons to follow their fathers onto the land, choosing instead to enter the army, the police, railway service and various industrial jobs, and for daughters to leave for domestic service (Report of Board of Agriculture, 1919, *25–9*; Armstrong, 1988, *111–16*).

Also long-term trends were moving against the interests of the labourer. Farm mechanization accounted for some reduction in the demand for labour after, rather than before, 1914, but its impact was less than changes in land-use. When farmers shifted from arable to grassland between 1870 and 1914 they required less labour, and indeed lower costs were one of the incentives for change. One complaint made by a number of writers at the end of the nineteenth century was that the best quality young people left the land and that 'only the dullards, the vicious, or the wastrels . . . unfitted for any other life' stayed behind (Haggard, 1902, 2, *539*). But F. M. L. Thompson has ironically observed, 'this collection of ageing cretins and village idiots must have performed wonders upon the land. Fewer of them produced more than their younger, sturdier, and more numerous forebears of the 1870s . . .' This is because the value of output remained roughly the same but as prices declined the physical volume of output was undoubtedly greater, even during the trough of depression in the 1890s, than in 1870 (Thompson, 1991, *219–20*). Thus the rise in real wages can be seen as a well-deserved increase in the individual worker's pitifully small share of income generated by agriculture (Horn, 1984b, *ch. 4*). It is difficult to say how much the individual farmworker benefited from this improvement. This is because although money wages were higher in the north and west, conditions of employment and retail prices of consumer goods also varied regionally. All workers gained from the decline in food prices, particularly of wheaten bread, but the gains from this source, as can be seen from Table 3, were greatest between 1873 and 1896. They were less after 1900 when prices recovered and farmworkers' wages lagged behind the rise in prices (Horn, 1984b, *217*). The benefits from lower wheat prices were also less in Scotland because of the higher consumption of oatmeal which fell less in price than wheat, and because Scottish labourers were more likely to receive part of their wages in kind (Orwin and Whetham, 1964, *218–19*; Mingay (ed.), 1981, 1, *86–7*; Keith, 1954, *96*; Mackie, 1992, *76, 108*).

Although emigration revived in the decade before the First World War, especially to Canada, the flight from the land, at least in England and Wales, slowed down in the Edwardian era. This was because the recovery of agricultural prices eased the squeeze on profits and so farmers did not seek the economies that lowered labour requirements as vigorously as they had done in the 1870s and 1880s (Orwin and Whetham, 1964, *231*; Armstrong, 1988, *115–16, 135*). But as output hardly fell and the numbers of farmers remained roughly unchanged, the substantial reduction in farm-workers meant a significant improvement in labour productivity. Between 1871 and 1911 output per worker increased by 26 per cent (Feinstein, 1972, *Tables 54 and 59*).

This loss of labour was a general feature and shows little regional correlation with the fortunes of farming. High-wage counties in the more prosperous livestock-producing north and west lost labour to industry and mining, and the low-wage counties of the depressed arable south-east suffered from the greater attractions of work in London (Hall, 1913). This indicates that pull was more important than push in explaining the movement (Orwin and Whetham, 1964, *343*). Transport developments played a part, although the national railway network was practically complete by 1870. In the 1900s the bicycle allowed young men to remain domiciled in one Huntingdon village but take jobs in the Peterborough brickworks (Haggar, 1902, 2, *94*).

No other country experienced such a transformation of its agriculture in the nineteenth century. The policies adopted in Britain contrasted with those followed in Europe (Tracy, 1989). Neither of the Royal Commissions was appointed as a prelude to any major measures of agricultural assistance. As so often occurs, they were a way of postponing any action until the immediate crisis that provoked agitation had passed. The legislation that followed the Richmond Commission did little to raise farmers' incomes. The second Agricultural Holdings Act in 1883 forced landlords to compensate a departing tenant for the value of unexhausted improvements he had made to the land. These included drainage work, the application of purchased fertilizers, and manure from animals fed on oil-cake. Although this was an improvement on the first Agricultural Holdings Act of 1875 which allowed both parties to contract out of this requirement, there were no universal standards for valuing such improvements so disputes could and did arise (Orwin and Whetham, 1964, *298–9*). The Settled Lands Acts, of 1882 and 1884, made it easier for landowners to get round the legal arrangements made by earlier generations (called entails) which required them to pass on the entire property to the eldest male heir. They could now sell part of the estate, without the expense of a Private Act of Parliament to do so, and use the money either to pay off debts or carry out improvements (Thompson, 1963, *319–20*; Fletcher, 1961a, *427*). The Board of Agriculture, established by William Pitt in 1793 in response to the Napoleonic Wars but dissolved in 1822, was recreated in 1889 and its President was given a place in the government (Ernle, 1912, *196*, *362*; Fletcher, 1916a, *427*). But as it was mainly concerned with coordinating legislation to control animal disease, collecting national agricultural statistics, and disseminating some educational material, it could provide little in the way of material assistance to farmers (Orwin and Whetham, 1964, *202*).

In the 1890s there was a further series of small measures that covered specific problems. The Fertilizers and Feeding Stuffs Act of 1893 gave farmers some consumer protection against manufacturers and merchants who sold them adulterated oil-cake and chemical manures (Ernle, 1912, *384*). The Market Gardeners Compensation Act, 1895, allowed tenants of holdings let as market gardens to claim compensation for all improvements they had made to the business, whether or not they had been made with the consent of the landlord. This covered fruit trees and bushes and the more permanent arable crops, such as asparagus, left behind at the end of their tenancy (Ernle, 1912, *384*; Orwin and Whetham, 1964, *299*). The 1896 Agricultural Rates Act, and subsequent Continuation Acts of 1901 onwards, relieved the owners and occupiers of farmland of some of the burden of local taxes (Ernle, 1912, *385*). However, local taxes only accounted for less than 2 per cent of total farming expenses (Dewey, 1984, *390*; Venn, 1933, *192–3*). The Improvement of Land Act of 1899 gave landowners increased facilities for carrying out improvements on borrowed money, but the government provided none of the actual money (Ernle, 1912, *384*).

Apart from these measures, governments of both political persuasions allowed the market to determine the size, structure, and health of the farm sector. The prospect of protection for wheat producers was never seriously discussed and, given the small weight of this enterprise even in the 1870s before the drastic price fall, it could not have provided much of a salvation for many farmers, unless the level had been high enough to exclude all imports and to encourage an expansion of acreage even higher than in 1870. Cormac Ó Gráda has calculated that the cost of a tariff of 18*s*. (90p) per quarter for wheat necessary to raise its price from the 32*s*. (£1 42p) per quarter average for the late 1880s and early 1890s to the 50*s*. (£2 50p) averaged in the early 1870s would have been £8.55 million. This was 5 per cent of all agricultural income in 1888–92, or 1 per cent of national income (Ó Gráda, 1981, *195–6*). Although this would have been a comparatively small transfer from the rest of the nation to agriculture, it would have benefited only a small part of the industry. Free trade in corn may only have been a symbol but it was fiercely defended whenever a return to protection was considered.

The British reaction contrasted sharply with that of many countries in Europe. In France there was a strong protectionist movement both within and outside Parliament. In 1881 this resulted in the introduction of a tariff on industrial goods, livestock and livestock products, but wheat was subject only to nominal duties, and other grains were exempt until 1885. As protectionist measures were in place before the difficulties of French agriculture became really serious with the price falls of the late 1880s, there was a strong basis for the extension of tariffs. Parliamentary debate was dominated by Jules Méline, a former Minister of Agriculture who had extended the duties of grain in 1885. In 1892 the 'Méline Tariff' strengthened the whole structure of industrial and agricultural protection. It imposed higher duties on barley, livestock, meat, cheese, wine, beer and hops and placed new duties on maize, rice, vegetables and potatoes, which had formerly entered free. The duties on agricultural products were between 10 per cent and 25 per cent of the value of those goods. But even these levels did not prevent continued imports of cheap food from forcing down French prices in the 1890s, so duties were raised again in 1894 and 1897 (Tracy, 1989, *65–9*). In France there was no reduction in either the value or volume of agriculture production before 1914, but food imports declined after 1894 and prices were higher (Tracy, 1989, *74, 76*). A comparison of British and French prices showed that in 1911–13 wheat, barley, oats and most livestock products were more expensive in France, although potatoes, cattle, and eggs still cost less. Cereal prices were highest with wheat more than 40 per cent more than in Britain, and as he could get a good price for this the French producer did not concentrate on livestock (Lamartine Yates, 1940, *256, 271*). France was able to impose these measures chiefly because agriculture was more important there; in 1881 only 18 per cent of British workers were employed in farming whereas in France it was 47 per cent (Feinstein, 1972, *Table 60*; Tracy, 1989, *77*). The protection of French agriculture remained in force beyond 1940, and may have been one reason why the French industrial sector remained smaller than the British because it prevented rationalization in agriculture and the transfer of labour to industry. French industry had some compensation from tariffs on manufactures, although these raised industrial prices for French farmers and caused some loss to them (Kindleberger, 1964, *280*). But the main costs of agricultural protection fell on French consumers, and apparently it was a price they were meekly prepared to pay.

Part of Britain's problem was that whereas the imports of wheat and flour increased by 110 per cent between 1870–4 and 1910–14, meat imports increased by 420 per cent and butter and cheese by 290 per cent (Fletcher, 1961a, *419*; Perren, 1978, *3*). Imports of cereals had not in themselves allowed an increase in *per capita* consumption, but imports of most other foodstuffs did. Any general scheme of protection might have severely reduced consumption of protein foods, whose prices had not declined disastrously, and upon which the rise in living standards before 1914 largely depended. Protection would also have affected the purchasing power of the primary producers, in whose markets Britain sold a considerable proportion of its exports of manufactures by 1914. As there were 6.5 million men working in industry in 1911, and only 1.3 million employed in agriculture, it made little sense to adopt measures that would reduce the demand for British goods abroad and purchasing power at home (Feinstein, 1972, *Table 60*; Orwin and Whetham, 1964, *342*). There were some restrictions on types of imports, such as the ban on imports of livestock, but this was done only to stop animal disease being brought into the country from abroad (Tracy, 1989, *45*; Perren, 1978, *157–8, 172–3*). Some Tory politicians flirted with the idea of limited protection, and Lord Salisbury adopted 'Fair Trade' in the 1880s, until the alliance with the Liberal Unionists forced the party to abandon it in 1891. Stronger protectionist feelings were aroused around the turn of the century when criticism over the Boer War left Britain without friends and the growth of German naval power provoked anxieties about the country's heavy reliance on imported food. The idea of Imperial Preference, which had been canvassed by Fair Traders, was espoused by Joseph Chamberlain and the Tariff Reform League. Their Tariff Commission produced a report on agriculture in 1906 that also stressed the dangers of reliance on imported food and advocated tariffs on foreign foodstuffs but the free entry into Britain of food from the Empire. But the election of 1906 produced a resounding defeat for the idea of any tax on food. It is doubtful if the League's proposals would have given much help to British farmers as they faced competition in temperate foodstuffs from both the Empire and foreign countries. If the latter had been excluded from the British market it would merely have encouraged Canada, Australia and New Zealand to expand production to fill the gap (see Table 1) left by Russia and America (Perry, 1974, *132*; Tracy, 1989, *45–7*).

For farmers who thought that agricultural education was one way to meet their problems, more opportunities became available. The Royal Agricultural College at Cirencester was founded in 1845 and intended for the sons of farmers (Orwin and Whetham, 1964, *163*). But there was little else before the Technical Instruction Act of 1889 empowered county councils to provide post-school agricultural education. Thereafter some councils, and also county agricultural associations, organized short courses delivered by travelling instructors, mostly in dairying subjects. Some counties combined to set up colleges or else agricultural departments within the existing universities. This was done and agricultural degrees were offered at Leeds, Newcastle, Bangor, Edinburgh, and Aberdeen universities (Perren, 1989, *265–6*; Orwin and Whetham, 1964, *281–2*). A number of counties, as well as some private benefactors, established their own residential agricultural colleges. The most famous of these were at Reading near London, at Kingston near Nottingham, at Newport near Stafford, at Newton Abbott in Devon, and at Whye in Kent (Orwin and Whetham, 1964, *376–7*). More money for agricultural education became available as some of these institutions were eligible for grants from the Board of Agriculture after 1889. After 1909 the financial situation was improved when the Liberal government's Development Fund Act set aside £2 million, and one of the purposes for which it could be used was agricultural education and research (Ernle, 1912, *437–8*). But these measures were never sufficient to amount to a national scheme before 1914, or after. The results could not compare with the organization provided in Denmark where the degree of state support was greater, although Britain was probably no worse than the rest of Europe (Lamartine Yates, 1940, *74–7, 541*; Orwin and Whetham, 1964, *377*). But most farmers and farmworkers before 1914 still learnt their trade by working with their fathers until they were old enough to move elsewhere.

However, the government gave no special encouragement for farmers to provide their own organizations to help them adapt to changed circumstances. In Europe, where farmers were more numerous and agriculture more important, they campaigned vigorously for other assistance beside protection, and their governments generally gave them satisfaction. In Britain there was a reluctance to realize the real nature of the threat from imports, and the prevalence of the landlord–tenant system made it difficult for agriculture to maintain a united front. The failure of British farmers to develop cooperatives in contrast to the success of the Danes, and to a lesser extent the French Agricultural Syndicates, was a further indication of either individualism or obstinacy (Tracy, 1989, *chs 3 and 5*). Even where adaptation took place farmers expected landlords to take the lead, in contrast with the situation before 1873 when farmers shared the initiative (Perren,

1970; Jones, 1962). C. P. Kindleberger has suggested a novel explanation of the slow switch from cereals to livestock. In his view livestock requires labour-intensive, capital-intensive small farms, in contrast to the land-intensive growing of wheat. To switch a tenant-farmed holding from cereals to livestock required the landlord to divide the farm, provide a second set of buildings and find a second farmer. Given the uncertainty as to future prices, landlords were unwilling to undertake investment on the scale this strategy required (Kindleberger, 1964, *245–7*). But Kindleberger's thesis conflicts with the fact that in Britain livestock farming required less labour than arable, so the shift from arable to livestock fitted in with the long-term decline in the agricultural workforce. His advocacy of more small animal farms apparently runs counter to this and suggests a reversal of the strategy adopted by those farmers and landlords who abandoned the high-cost production methods of high farming. However, there is evidence, both before and after 1914, that some enterprising farmers were prepared to adapt premises for dairying and other purposes at their own expense rather than get into long-drawn-out negotiations with the landlord (Channing, 1897, *134–6*; Mackie, 1992, *77*; Keith, 1954, *31*).

4
Temporary revival, 1914–1921

The first measures introduced after the outbreak of war in August 1914 tended to work against agriculture's food-producing interests. At that time the President of the Board of Agriculture saw 'no occasion whatever for public alarm over food supplies'. Yet the enlistment of tens of thousands of men from the agricultural districts, army requisitioning of thousands of horses and tons of fodder, and the rise in prices and reduced supplies of imported foodstuffs and fertilizers all placed pressure on the level of output from British farms (Horn, 1984a; Armstrong, 1991, *111–15*; Whetham, 1978, *70–5*). By the summer of 1915, retail food prices had risen by a third of their pre-war level, and by June 1916 they were some 60 per cent above the 1914 level. Disquiet over rising food prices and the lack of a policy for increasing home production led the government to appoint a committee in May 1915 to report on what measures would be desirable to increase the output of England and Wales if the war were to continue beyond the harvest of 1916 (Dewey, 1989, *24–5*). This committee, under the chairmanship of Lord Milner, produced an interim report in July 1915. After emphasizing the inevitable time-lag between any decision to produce more cereals and the eventual delivery of increased output, it pointed out that extra grain crops could only be produced by abandoning existing rotations and also ploughing up existing grassland. Farmers would find both measures costly and they would only freely incur these costs if they were given a guarantee of assured prices and markets for some years into the future (Whetham, 1978, *76*).

The government rejected this proposal in August 1915, arguing that the situation did not require commitments that could seriously add to the financial problems in post-war years. The decision was understandable as the harvest in Britain and America promised to be large and the threat to imports receded as the German submarine campaign seemed to be on the wane. The Milner Committee issued its final report in October 1915, taking note of the government's decision but pointing out the need to increase the productivity of the soil and that land could produce twice as much meat and milk when under the plough than when in permanent grass, as well as producing corn for human consumption. The Board of Agriculture suggested that farmers should increase their output of wheat, oats, potatoes, milk, bacon, and cheese but warned them that no financial inducements would be offered by the government since it believed the higher prices already dominating the markets were adequate to cover any increase in costs. Policy was only changed, and farmers offered financial inducements to expand the acreage of cereals, when the 1916 harvest turned out to be a poor one and an intensified submarine campaign put pressure on food imports (Dewey, 1989, *26–33*). In December 1916 a new government was appointed, with a Food Controller in its ranks, and its policy was now to increase the home supply of grain and potatoes. Since the report of the Milner Committee two other committees, the Hobhouse Committee and the Selbourne Committee, had both urged the government either during or after the war to guarantee minimum prices for two grain crops, and to ensure that the area of arable land was increased (Whetham, 1978, *77, 83–7*). A food production programme was hurriedly put together early in 1917. Farmers were given guaranteed minimum prices for wheat and oats for six years – barley was omitted out of deference to the temperance movement – the position to be reviewed after four years, in 1920. During the existence of guaranteed prices there were to be minimum wages for agricultural workers enforced by wages boards. Owners and tenants of agricultural land were to be required to follow cropping directions issued by the agricultural departments, to ensure the use of land in the national interest. There should be no increase in rents as a result of the maintenance of minimum prices (Whetham, 1978, *91*).

These measures were included in the Corn Production Act of August 1917 which extended the period of guaranteed prices of wheat and oats, on a descending scale, up to 1922; guaranteed prices were 60s. per quarter for wheat and 38s. 6d. for oats. If implemented, the minimum prices involved a deficiency payment, equal to the deficiency by which the annual average market price fell below the minimum, for every acre returned as under wheat or oats, assuming that the average yield was four quarters of wheat per acre and five quarters of oats. This method of guaranteeing farmers' incomes, first introduced in 1917, of deficiency payments with guaranteed prices, became an important feature of government agricultural policy, and was used again in the interwar years and after 1945 (Brown, 1991, *187*). The same Act set up the Agricultural Wages Board which fixed minimum wage rates at 25s. a week. Neither the minimum prices nor the minimum wages ever operated as wartime shortages forced prices and wages far above these levels (Ernle, 1912, *415–16*; Whetham, 1978, *94–7*).

The government, by guaranteeing cereal prices in 1917, reversed its earlier policies and encouraged arable at the expense of livestock farming. Up to the end of 1916 agriculture had been left to operate largely within the pre-war *laissez faire* framework. The main changes affecting farmers' incomes were the partial cessation of foreign competition, and the rise in the demand for farm products created by full employment. From 1917 onwards agriculture became a controlled industry with government direction of production, while at the same time the marketing of farm products became essentially a government monopoly, and the consumer was protected by price and other forms of control. The wartime years saw a great increase in farmers' profits and the real return on their capital grew continuously for most of the war. Highest rates of growth were achieved in 1914–15 when the industry was uncontrolled, and profits reached their absolute peak in 1917 before falling back slightly in 1918. The reason for the increase was that although prices rose this was not matched by the increase in costs. For the first three years of the war agricultural wages failed to keep pace with inflation, lagging seriously behind the rise in farm prices (Horn, 1984a, *192–3*). On many farms the wages bill fell as men joined the armed forces, so labour costs rose at roughly the same rate as total costs until 1918 when the wages bill received a large boost. Rent was static because landlords were reluctant to face the charge of wartime profiteering and may also have been slow to accept high wartime inflation as permanent. When inflation had become an established fact the 1917 Corn Production Act effectively banned any rent increase. The price of purchased feedstuffs rose faster than the average of total costs but feedstuff usage had roughly halved by 1918 (Dewey, 1984). In some instances the government provided particular assistance to farmers. In the early stages of the war it saw shortage of labour as one obstacle to increased production. An acre of arable land required approximately 9.25 times as much labour as an acre of grassland (Dewey, 1975, *112*). The extra manpower required was sometimes used as an argument against proposals to increase corn production by ploughing up pasture, even though there were comparatively small losses of labour in 1915 and 1916 (Dewey, 1989, *56*). But in the later stages the use of prisoners of war and the Women's Land Army provided farmers with official supplies of extra labour which also undercut the farmworker's bargaining position (Whetham, 1964; Armstrong, 1991). As a recognition of this fact the 1917 Corn Product Act set a minimum wage of 25s. a week and also created a Central Agricultural Wages Board which was operating in England and Wales by the middle of 1918 (Armstrong, 1988, *166*). In Scotland there was satisfaction with the existing system of voluntary negotiating committees and therefore no wages board was set up there.

The net effect of the war on production was to interrupt the pre-1914 concentration on livestock although as can be seen from Table 5, there was no radical change until 1917–18. There was an expansion of the area of tillage in Britain, mostly in England and Wales, from 10.3 million acres in 1913 to 12.4 million in 1918 at the expense of a reduction in permanent grassland from 17.5 million to 15.9 million and in temporary grass from 4.0 million to 3.5 million acres (MAFF, 1968, *95–7*). Although the value of the four main items of agricultural output shown in Table 5, accounting for some 70 per cent of total output (Dewey, 1989, *247*), was some 11 per cent lower in 1918 than in 1909–13 this is somewhat misleading because it involved a shift from high value outputs (meat and milk) to low value outputs (cereals and potatoes) whose prices were controlled by the government in 1917 and 1918. A better measure of the success of the wartime food policy is provided by estimates of how much more of the nation's food

Table 5 *England and Wales: value of output sold off farms, 1914–18 (£ million, in 1909–13 prices)*

	1909–13	1914	1915	1916	1917	1918
Cereals[a]	21.5	22.8	22.6	20.6	21.5	29.4
Potatoes	9.1	10.0	9.7	8.5	11.3	14.3
Meat	56.1	55.8	53.5	55.6	48.6	37.5
Milk	38.6	41.4	39.1	36.7	34.2	30.5
Totals	125.3	130.0	124.9	121.4	115.6	111.7
As per cent	100	104	100	97	92	89

[a] Wheat, oats, barley.
Source: Dewey, 1975, *105*.

supply was produced by British agriculture in 1918 than in 1914. In the 1920s it was believed that this had risen from 34 to 42 per cent (Middleton, 1923, *322*). However, recent research by P. E. Dewey has shown that the achievement was more modest. He estimates that British farmers supplied 38 per cent of the food consumed in 1914, but with the food production campaign they only raised this to 40 per cent by 1918. He also estimates that in 1918 imports provided only 53 per cent of food and that the other 7 per cent was gained from food control measures (Dewey, 1989, *227*). These involved the better use of all foodstuffs and the prevention of unnecessary waste. By 1918 there were, for example, regulations that compelled millers to extract more flour from the wheat they processed, and a prohibition on feeding livestock with grain suitable for human consumption (Dewey, 1989, *225–6*).

Britain's wartime experience differed from the rest of Europe in that she was the only country whose government took effective steps to revive agricultural production. This was in sharp contrast to Germany where, in the face of the Allied naval blockade, wartime agriculture failed to maintain peacetime levels of output and the government was forced to resort to permanent food rationing from the summer of 1916 onwards (Offer, 1989, *26–31*). In contrast, serious food rationing was not needed in Britain until 1918 (Horn, 1984a, 155, *190–1*). The main reason for the differing nutritional experiences of the two populations was the breaking of the German blockade by the use of the convoy system for merchant ships on the vital north Atlantic route, and an effective imposition of a blockade on Germany. Nevertheless, in 1917–18 the military measures had some modest support from the limited success of the food production campaign, and rather more from the food control measures. A larger increase in output was not achieved because British farmers still faced problems, particularly shortages of labour, chemical fertilizers and animal feed (Dewey, 1991, *252–4*). The war imbued all classes with a sense of uncertainty and in spite of A. G. Street's statement that 'It was impossible to lose money at farming just then' anxiety remained about the future (Street, 1932, *201*; Horn, 1984a, *183–6*). The wartime revival of cultivation was not a permanent feature and after it had reached its peak in 1918, as there was little confidence in the prospects of tillage farming, much of the newly ploughed land reverted to pasture in 1919–21 (Middleton, 1923, *333–4*). One way in which the wartime prosperity also acted as a destabilizing force was in its impact on the behaviour of landowners. Many landlords were disillusioned by their unprofitable experiences since 1879 and made nervous by Lloyd George's 'people's budget' in 1910 with its increased taxation and death duties (Perren, 1989, *252–3*). They had begun to sell even before 1914 and in some cases they were prompted to sell in the latter stages of the war by the desire to adjust the scale of their landholdings 'while the going was good and the market land-hungry' (Thompson, 1963, *335*). If they had raised rents the increment would have been liable to income or supertax, whereas none was payable on the capital proceeds of the sale of farms (Armstrong, 1991, *130*).

5

Depression of the 1920s and 1930s

In the months just after the Armistice in November 1918 agriculture was still as closely controlled as in the last weeks of hostilities. In January 1919 there was the bizarre case where an 81-year-old woman farmer in Essex was fined the substantial sum of £227 for using wheat to feed poultry in defiance of wartime regulations prohibiting the feeding of livestock with grain suitable for human consumption (Horn, 1984a, 66–7). Many farmers, unused to keeping records or even to following any directions in cultivating their holdings, other than their own inclinations and perhaps the landlord's covenants, hated the controls associated with wartime regulations. Even some of the County War Agricultural Executive Committees, which had been responsible for implementing and enforcing policy at the local level since the beginning of 1917, had begun to resent the endless stream of directives to which they were subjected (Whetham, 1978, 97–102, 118–19; Horn, 1984a, 67–8). In the immediate aftermath of the war agricultural prices rose sharply, by 26 per cent between 1918 and 1921 (Whetham, 1978, 230). This was the result of poor crops in 1919–20, of serious shortages caused by economic disruption in post-war Europe, and of the immediate post-war boom when full employment fuelled demand and pushed up prices. The international wheat situation worsened in the early months of 1920 when the Argentinian government announced an embargo on exports of grain for a year, and there was a poor Australian crop (Astor and Murray, 1933, 48). Against this background the need for any special price measures to protect farmers' interests was questioned in some quarters. During the war two measures had been in operation, the one of price support and the other of price control. Farmers confused their loathing of price control with price support, as the support policy had lain dormant with the high prices during and immediately after the war (Brown, 1989, *78*). But farmers' lobbyists needed to be reassured that the industry would not once again be left to the vagaries of the peacetime market, as their public voice had become much stronger during the war. The National Farmers' Union had grown since its beginning in Lincolnshire in 1908 to claim 80,000 members in 48 branches in 1918 and the status of a truly national negotiating body (Whetham, 1978, *129*).

In July 1919 the question of post-war agricultural policy was remitted to a Royal Commission (RC Interim Report, 1919). This was asked to report as soon as possible on cereal prices, leaving other matters until later. At the end of the year it submitted three reports, a majority report signed by twelve members, a minority report signed by eleven members, and a third report signed by one member. The minority report decided that guaranteed prices for cereals were unnecessary, but the majority report advocated guaranteed prices for all cereals as a method of ensuring that some of the grassland ploughed during the war remained in tillage and was cultivated in proper rotation. The third report, signed by one member (Lord Cautley), recommended that as long as minimum wages for workers were enforced on farmers, there should be minimum prices for cereals, to encourage farmers to employ the existing labour force (Whetham, 1978, *119–20*).

The government followed the main recommendations of the majority report and passed the Agriculture Act in December 1920 which replaced the price guarantees of the 1917 Corn Production Act. Minimum prices for wheat and oats were to be maintained and farmers would be given four years' notice of any decision to withdraw them; the level of guarantees, based on average prices in 1919, was raised to 68*s.* per quarter (c. 495 lb) for wheat and 46*s.* for oats, although barley was once again omitted. The new guaranteed prices were to operate from the beginning of the cereal year in August 1921. The debate over the Agriculture Bill dragged on from May to December and the irony of the situation was that once the Act was passed its economic justification disappeared. The resumption of massive grain imports from Argentina, Canada, Australia and India meant a severe fall in the prices of cereals in 1921. In June 1921 wheat fetched 89*s.* 3*d.* per quarter but plummeted to 45*s*. 8*d*. in December (Cooper, 1989, *53–4*). The acreage of British wheat was still high in 1921; although it had fallen somewhat from its peak in 1918 it was, at 2,041,000 acres, some 20 per cent above its 1913 level. The situation was not so serious for oats: its peak in 1918 was 4024 acres and this had declined 21 per cent by 1921, so it was then only 9 per cent above its level in 1913 (MAFF, 1968, *98, 100*). Although the disastrous fall in cereal prices was exactly the sort of emergency both the Corn Production and the Agriculture Act had been designed to meet, the government, beset by worsening conditions in the whole economy, was unwilling to incur the enhanced cost of this particular piece of legislation. It was estimated the Act would involve it in payments of around £20 million to agriculture which was a minor activity, whilst at the same time it had refused to assist more important industries in the face of worsening economic depression. In 1921 unemployment reached the then record level of 12.2 per cent of the total workforce, which both sharply reduced the tax base and increased the cost of unemployment insurance (Feinstein, 1972, *Table 58, 14, 12*). It was therefore not surprising the cabinet should decide on June 2 that it could not afford to implement the guaranteed minimum prices, and authorized the Minister of Agriculture to announce the repeal which followed in August. In the event compensation grants were given in 1922, based on the planted acreages of wheat and oats in 1921. Payments of £3 per acre for wheat and £4 per acre for oats were made, amounting to £15,000,000 in England and Wales and £4,400,000 in Scotland (Whetham, 1978, *140*; Ernle, 1912, *417*).

The immediate reaction of the agricultural lobby to the abandonment of the guarantees was largely favourable. During the winter of 1920 farmers felt cheated by the Ministry of Food buying wheat for about 10*s*. a quarter less than the 95*s*. a quarter the Prime Minister had promised to maintain. The farmers reckoned they would be better off without controls even if the price of corn fell from its present heights. Most of the wartime increase in the wheat and oats acreage had already disappeared and by 1920 it was down to 5,233,000 acres as opposed to the peak of 6,660,000 in 1918 and 4,717,000 in 1914 (MAFF, 1968, *93, 98, 100*). When the government offered that freedom, they believed they would gain more from the abolition of controls over markets and the suspension of the Agricultural Wages Board, than they would lose from the removal of price guarantees (Brown, 1989, *78–9*).

Nevertheless, a phrase used in connection with the government's action was 'Great Betrayal', which was employed by E. H. Whetham in an article in 1974 (Whetham, 1974). However, this article emphasizes the discontent with the system of controls that had emerged during the war years and the partial nature of any betrayal. The two features of the 1921 repeal most heavily criticized in Parliament were the loss of the four years' notice to allow farmers time to return their land to a proper system of rotation, and the likelihood that in the future it would impede cooperation and trust between farmers, landlords, and the Ministry of Agriculture (Whetham, 1974, *48*). The same point about partial betrayal is made more strongly by A. F. Cooper (Cooper, 1986, 1989, *42–63*). He points out that agriculture in the 1920s contained (as it did before 1914) a diversity of social and economic interests. The public figures – landowners like Lord Milner, Lord Bledisloe and Christopher Turnor – who had been vociferous advocates of increased home production, more land under the plough, and the regeneration of agriculture by state assistance, were expressing a different point of view to the National Farmers' Union, who opposed any state regulation of wages (Cooper, 1986, *102–3*). The feeling of betrayal was one that arose in the later 1920s as the situation worsened, and as more farmers, in addition to the limited number of corn growers, felt the effects of increased competition and declining prices. Against this background they were, not unnaturally, inclined to look back on the immediate post-war period as an all too brief golden era. G. M. Robinson comments: 'This "Great Betrayal" of British farming led to a difficult decade for farmers' (Robinson, 1988, *146*). But the primary reason for their difficulties was the low prices caused by world surpluses of all internationally traded agricultural products and not the decision of the British government to abandon its price guarantees for wheat and oats, which accounted for only a small part of total output.

Farmers who had been established in 1914 and had invested their wartime gains in securities unconnected with farming may have had some protection from the price fall of the 1920s, as they at least still had some profits to lose. Those in the weakest position were returning soldiers needing to restock at the high prices ruling after the war (Venn, 1933, *516–17*; Street, 1932, *209–12*). At the same time landowners continued the process begun after 1909 of selling substantial parts of their estates. There was a demand for land from town businessmen who had made fortunes during the war and wished to retire and enjoy the pleasures of rural life. This demand for land, in contrast to the situation in the 1880s when landowners who wanted to sell found it impossible to get rid of their estates, was a further encouragement for landlords to sell. It is estimated that between 1918 and 1921 perhaps a quarter of the land of England changed hands (Thompson, 1963, *336*; Horn, 1984a, *203*). This was often to sitting tenants, so that many farmers were saddled with large mortgages incurred during years of high prices but which had to be serviced in following years when prices were much lower.

The twenty years and ten months between the Armistice of November 1918 and the outbreak of war in September 1939 was generally an unprofitable period for British farmers. Profits had come too easily during the rise in prices between 1914 and 1919. From May 1920 the general level of wholesale prices began to fall, and fell for eighteen months to reach a level barely half that recorded at the peak. Linked to world markets by its sales, as well as by its purchases of feedstuffs, fertilizers and petrol, British agriculture shared with other industries the results of the general price fall that followed the post-war boom. In 1920 and 1921 those who bought to sell again, particularly farmers who purchased store stock to sell as fatstock, could not help making a profit because prices were always higher when they came to sell. But the precipitate fall in prices from the spring of 1921 to the spring of 1923 meant that no farmer could avoid making a loss as prices were always lower than when he incurred his costs (Whetham, 1978, *142*; Street, 1923, *206–9*).

In the 1920s the trend in agricultural prices was downwards, interrupted by periods of relative stability from 1923 to 1925 and again from 1927 to 1929. British farmers were once more exposed to the effects of foreign competition, without the protection of wartime conditions and government financial assistance. Throughout the decade British agriculture was feeling the effects of overseas competition which for some products was even more severe than that experienced between 1870 and 1914. World trade in wheat and wheat flour rose from an annual average of 644 million bushels in 1909–13 to 833 million in 1924–8 while trade in feed grains increased from 259 million bushels to 329 million. There was some relief for British corn growers as between 1911–13 and 1925–9 annual average imports of grain and meal, excluding wheat, into this country declined by about 24 per cent while those of wheat remained about the same. But as Britain was the largest market, taking over 27 per cent of world wheat exports and over 20 per cent of feed grains the effect of the increased world supply exerted strong pressures on prices in this country (Taylor and Taylor, 1943, *125, 146*). For the livestock sector the 1920s saw a direct intensification of competition and imports of meat rose by 44 per cent, butter imports by 59 per cent and cheese by 28 per cent (Astor and Rowntree, 1938, *34, 113*).

But it is not always easy to tell just how serious were the effects of depression on farmers. Investigations undertaken by correspondents for *The Times* in 1922 alleged that 'farmers of all classes, in all districts, are in serious financial straits' and mentioned 'losses of £5 per acre in Norfolk' and the state of northern farmers as 'far worse than that of forty years ago'. Nevertheless, it is as hazardous to generalize from such extreme statements after 1920 as it is to do so between 1873 and 1896. This can be seen if we do as Perry did for 1871–93 and take farm bankruptcies as an indicator of distress. During the years 1914–20 bankruptcies and deeds of arrangement among farmers in England and Wales averaged 82 per annum: in 1921 they rose to 285 and to 403 in 1922. For the rest of the decade they averaged 496 per annum before climbing to 497 and 560 in 1931 and 1932 and dropping back to 428 in 1933; from 1934 to 1939 farmer bankruptcies averaged only 240 per annum. We can see there is no doubt that the absolute number of bankruptcies rose, but in the 1920s this was equivalent only to one farmer in 530, and even in 1932 to only one in 440. The agricultural economist J. A. Venn, writing in 1933, believed the statements of 'widespread bankruptcies' among farmers that appeared at various times in the interwar press were obviously wild exaggerations (Venn, 1933, *520, 542, 567*; Sturmey, 1968, *302*). This also means that J. R. Bellerby's statement that the years 1923–9 were ones that gave rise to 'conditions verging on bankruptcy for much of British agriculture' needs to be qualified

(Bellerby, 1968, *73*). There is no doubt that farmers' earnings were depressed and, relative to those outside agriculture, were seriously reduced in these years, but in both cases their level was higher than in the depression years of the 1880s and 1890s and at no time before 1940 were they ever depressed enough to cause a widespread exodus (Bellerby, 1968, *56*; Feinstein, 1972, *Table 23*). The number of farmers in Great Britain was 316,000 in 1921, and this fell by 7 per cent to 294,000 in 1931, but by 1951 (when the next Census was taken) had recovered to 302,000 (Taylor, 1955, *40*).

Some districts and kinds of soils, linked to certain specializations, were far more subject to depression than others. The low prices of the 1920s gave rise to renewed pressure on arable farmers. Profits were possible in the mid-1920s when prices stabilized to some extent, even in arable farming, but these were small enough to be wiped out by interest and management charges; they were certainly never large enough to recoup the losses of 1922 and 1923 (Brown, 1989, *80*). It may seem surprising that, with prices generally higher than they were before 1914, the 1920s should have been a time of such difficulty. Although the precipitous decline in prices ended in 1922 the problem was that there was no recovery after then and prices continued to drift slowly down over most of the 1920s (Venn, 1933, *534*). The largest decline was in cereals, followed by fatstock, butter and cheese; the price of liquid milk was generally the most buoyant of all the major agricultural commodities (Cohen, 1936, *67*; Keith, 1954, *105*). Although the minor commodities, such as fruit, vegetables and potatoes, gave higher returns their prices were much more volatile. As a response more farms in midland and eastern England turned to growing vegetables, especially the bulky winter vegetables which utilized manure from livestock on the same holdings (Robinson, 1983, *60*; 1988, *117*). But they did not account for a large share of agricultural output, amounting to around 10 per cent in the 1920s and 1930s (Ojala, 1952, *209*), and as they were grown mostly by market gardeners and smallholders, they could only offer a refuge for a comparatively small number of farmers.

The effects of declining prices would not have been serious had farmers been able to achieve a proportionate reduction in their costs, but as many of these were inflexible in a downwards

direction real costs tended to rise. J. Brown believes it was the
inability to keep costs in line with prices that was responsible for
many of agriculture's problems in the 1920s and 1930s (Brown,
1991, *195*). This was particularly the case with labour costs; under
wartime conditions and the Central Agricultural Wages Board,
farmworkers' wages had risen to a peak of 46*s.* a week in August
1920. Even before this body was abolished in October 1921 it was
negotiating a reduction of minimum wages to 42*s.* a week in 34
counties. The Corn Production (Repeal) Act of 1921 set up
voluntary County Conciliation Committees composed of farmers
and workers, but they proved to be a dead letter. Employers
reverted to the pre-war practice of individual farm negotiations and
by 1922 wages had fallen to an average figure of around 28*s.* a
week, although levels were higher (35*s.*) in northern counties and
lower (25*s.*) in East Anglia. Attempts at further reductions by
farmers in Norfolk, a corn-growing county that was badly hit by
the decline in cereal prices, provoked a serious strike there in
March and April 1923. Against this background the first Labour
government brought forward a bill to restore statutory wage
regulation in agriculture and the Agricultural Wages (Regulation)
Act followed in 1924. Under this measure, local control was
placed in the hands of County Committees, consisting of equal
numbers of representatives of farmworkers' organizations and the
NFU. At the level of the individual farm it was always difficult to
monitor whether agreed minimum rates were enforced, and there
were many ways that employers underpaid. But this machinery was
one factor that prevented the level of wages from falling further.
Average minimum levels for ordinary workers rose from 28*s.* in
1924 to 31*s.* 5*d.* the following year. Thereafter they remained
remarkably steady, with only small losses in 1931-32, before rising
to 34*s.* 9*d.* in 1939. Scotland had no wages legislation until 1937,
and a comparison of rates in England and Wales with those of
Scotland shows that the unregulated Scottish rates moved ad-
versely to the English and Welsh in the decade after 1924
(Armstrong, 1988, *180–3*). However, the poorer wages record of
Scotland is also likely to have been influenced by the lower
productivity of its farming and fewer opportunities for workers
there to move out of agriculture.

During the depression of 1873–96 labour had accounted for 20–

25 per cent of expenses. In the 1920s only small farms relying on family labour were able to keep their labour bill as low as this. On other farms labour usually accounted for 25–30 per cent of farm costs, and sometimes it was more (Brown, 1989, *83–4*). In 1931 a survey covering approximately a thousand arable farms in eastern England revealed that labour was 37.7 per cent of outgoings, which made it the largest single item. Before 1920 livestock, feedstuffs, machinery and manures had accounted for over half of all farm costs but in 1931 they only came to 35.7 per cent on these farms (Venn, 1933, *249*). The general fall in the price of purchased manures and the cost of feedstuffs was some benefit to farmers, as was the decline of rents. In the case of rent per acre this fell after 1922 and up to 1939 by approximately 20 per cent, but the decline was itself a reflection of agricultural depression. In the early 1930s rents varied from £2 per acre for rich fenland farms and market gardens near to towns down to a few shillings on hill land and exceptionally light or heavy soils (Whetham, 1978, *137, 159–60, 263–4*). However, the sale of land after the war, mostly to sitting tenants, which raised the percentage of holdings in England and Wales farmed by owner-occupiers from 11 to 36 per cent, meant fewer farmers were able to benefit from lower rents (Sturmey, 1968, *287*). Many farmers were reluctant to purchase but had little choice if the owner threatened to put the farm on the open market if they refused (Street, 1932, *201–2*). In December 1920 the tenants on Sir Beville Stanier's 4000 acre Peplow estate in Shropshire unsuccessfully petitioned him not to sell (Perren, 1989, *254*). Farmers who bought their holdings, unless they could do so out of wartime profits, had to rely on bank overdrafts. They no doubt hoped the return to reasonable profitability of pre-war years would enable them to service these debts. When prices fell catastrophically they found this very hard to do; whereas landlords' response to hard times was to allow the accumulation of arrears and grant reductions, banks were not so understanding (Brown, 1989, *85–6*).

Farmers found that their share of agricultural income was squeezed (see Table 6) and reacted to depression as they did in the 1870s, by looking for ways to reduce costs. The higher cost of labour to the farmer stimulated those types of farming that gave a high return per man employed – dairying, intensive production of pigs, eggs or vegetables, together with mechanized grain growing

Table 6 *Agricultural output and shares of farm income, 1920–39*

	Gross agricultural output (£ million at 1911–13 prices)			Share of farm income (per cent)		
	Crops	Livestock	Total output	Wages	Rent	Farmers' income
1920–2	57.81	153.28	211.09	36	16	48
1924–9	47.56	132.37	179.83	43	24	33
1930–4	45.23	142.04	187.27	40	23	37
1935–9	46.83	138.87	185.70	37	19	44

Sources: Output, Ojala, 1952, *209*; Income, Feinstein, 1972, *Table 23*.

on easily worked soils. The mixed family farm also showed its survival value; at the expense of a low standard of living, the unit could outlast temporary fluctuations in prices. Labour productivity rose at around 1 per cent per annum in the 1920s before increasing to 2.2 per cent in the 1930s (Robinson, 1988, *148*). It can also be seen from Table 6 that there was a continuation of the emphasis on livestock farming, and in the bid to reduce costs cheap feedstuffs were of primary importance to the dairy farmer, to the specialist producer of pigs and eggs, and to a lesser extent to the grazier who sold fat cattle. Even in the predominantly arable districts, the tendency in the interwar years was to increase the output of livestock products by the greater use of purchased feedstuffs, and to devote the fields to cash crops such as wheat, barley, potatoes, sugar beet and vegetables rather than to the production of fodder crops. Costs were further reduced by concentrating attention on only that land and those tasks that paid. Thus nettles were allowed to grow in awkward corners of fields, while scrub was allowed to advance up some of the Berkshire downs and take over many fields on the heavy Essex claylands (Astor and Rowntree, 1938, *38*).

But the precarious balance achieved between 1924 and 1929 was again undermined by the renewed fall in cereal prices that heralded the Great Depression of the 1930s. The world economic depression of 1929–32, with its chronic surpluses of primary products, had a severe effect on Britain's farmers as the home market was unprotected by tariffs and so became a dumping ground for numerous farm products. The United Kingdom entered the world crisis in 1929 with high state-regulated wages for agricultural labourers, a large number of unemployed, and a large import surplus of goods. The latter was only partly met by its exports of goods and services and the dividends paid by British investments overseas. With increased protection for agriculture on the continent of Europe, more and more crops produced for world trade crowded into the markets of the remaining free-trade countries. These increased imports also appeared dangerous from the standpoint of the currency, since receipts from services and capital investments also dropped substantially. In October 1931 the volume of food imports was 35 per cent above normal (Tracy, 1989, *150*). Under the pressure of great gold losses by the Bank of England, the pre-war parity of the pound sterling, which had been restored in April 1925, was abandoned in September 1931. Its depreciation perceptibly lightened the burdens of many debtors, and at the same time raised the price of imports, which enabled English farmers to compete more successfully with foreign producers (Taylor and Taylor, 1943, *246*).

At no time in the interwar years was the British market a healthy one for farm products as rising incomes and population growth were greatly reduced from the high rates achieved before 1914. Between 1870–4 and 1909–13 *per capita* consumption of meat had increased from 108 lb to 135 lb but by 1934 it had only risen to 143 lb, while *per capita* consumption of wheat flour actually declined after 1913 (Perren, 1978, *3*; Orr, 1938, *18*). Between the wars there was a wider range of products from which the consumer could choose. This meant that instead of farmers being able to depend on pre-war growth rates in consumption after 1920 they had to fight even harder for market shares wherever there were foreign substitutes for their products (Capie, 1978, *52–3*). As in the 1920s, farms with substantial sales of grain were the first to be affected by depression after 1930, particularly those on heavy soils where cultivations and field drainage were costly. On cheap feedstuffs livestock enterprises flourished for a time, until falling demand and increasing foreign and domestic supplies affected those prices as well. The price index of farm crops compiled by the Ministry of Agriculture sank from 106.5 (1927–9 = 100) in 1928 to 74 in 1930, and to 71 in 1933; the prices of livestock and livestock products (on the same base period) showed little change in 1929 and 1930, but fell sharply in subsequent years to 75 in 1933 (Tracy, 1989, *159*).

The gradual recovery of agricultural profits from 1932 onwards was aided by various measures described in chapter 6 below, and also by the general recovery of world prices. The depression brought considerable changes in the structure of British agriculture, which adjusted itself to produce a larger quantity of the more profitable foods – livestock products and vegetables. But the performance of the sector as a whole was unspectacular, and the agricultural output of the UK was roughly constant, rising by 1.6 per cent between 1928–9 and 1936–7 (Feinstein, 1972, Table 8). In the ten years before the Second World War, the number of regular full-time workers employed in British agriculture fell from 729,000 to 601,000, or by 17.5 per cent; the fall was proportionately largest for women and for youths (MAFF, 1968, *62*). The pull of competing employments, offering higher wages, shorter hours and better housing, and the push of farm mechanization combined to reduce the number employed on the land while raising output per man by 40 per cent between 1924 and 1939 (Armstrong, 1988, *179, 195, 197, 199–201*). The progress of farm mechanization, which had been slow in the 1920s, advanced more after 1930. Tractors became commoner in arable districts in the south-east; the number in England and Wales rose from 14,565 in 1925 to 16,000 in 1930 and by 1938 there were some 40,000, mostly on holdings of over 300 acres; only after 1940 did they become a truly irresistible force (Whetham, 1978, *210*; Collin, 1983, *73*). Combine harvesters, crop sprayers, milking machines, row-crop cultivators and a host of other labour-saving devices were tried, modified and adopted by a few progressive farmers. The standard of agricultural education, although organized in a haphazard manner and used by a minority of farmers and workers, was nevertheless improved. Milk recording, improved strains of crops, bull licensing to eliminate the worst animals, more accurate knowledge of soils and manuring, and the prevention of diseases and pests, all led to lower costs and higher output per man (Astor and Rowntree, 1938, *403–24*).

Such prosperity as was thus attained was based largely on livestock and their products. Milk, cattle, pigs, poultry and eggs were, in that order, the most important sources of farm income and probably of farm profits too. Sales of milk in Great Britain were valued at £68 million in 1937–8; potatoes, the most valuable farm crop, brought in some £14.5 million, while the sales of wheat totalled only £9 million, including subsidy. In the autumn of 1938 there were about 110,000 milk producers registered under the Milk Marketing Boards, which did not cover Northern Ireland or the whole of Scotland; in comparison some 76,650 farmers in the whole of Great Britain were registered as growers of wheat. The decline in the area of tillage was relatively least in Scotland and the old arable districts of the east and north-east of England; it was relatively greatest in the other areas where, even before 1914, crops had been comparably less important. Mixed farming – arable cultivation with a cycle of corn, root crops and leys of grass or clover – gave way over much of England and Wales to other types of farming. Some districts saw the further displacement of cheese-making, butter-making and now cattle fattening by the relentless rise of liquid milk production. In the west and midlands there was the all-grass dairy or stock farm; open-air dairying with movable milking sheds was adopted in the dry chalk uplands of southern England, where cows were fed on cattle-cake and grass. In eastern districts milk production was increasingly combined with sugar beet and other crops for sale. The all-grass farm lost the machinery and traditions of cultivation; its land, acquiring fertility from cake-fed animals, tended to become 'cow-sick' and to deteriorate in feeding value. The outlying or intractable fields of arable farms were apt to follow the same trend and to become indifferent grass or to lie derelict (Maxton, 1936; Whetham, 1978).

The view that British farming was undercapitalized in the interwar years has been expressed by a number of authors, writing both at the time and since (Astor and Rowntree, 1938, *384*; Whetham, 1978, *172, 197, 283–4*; Brown, 1989, *84–5, 123*). This needs some explanation as low prices made the average return on invested capital from most farms, particularly small farms, well below rates obtainable in other sectors of the economy and lower than farmers had to pay the banks for loans (Astor and Rowntree, 1938, *385*). As the average return on farming capital was so low there seems little justification for extra investment to drive marginal returns even lower. Also British farmers had relatively more capital than their counterparts in Europe (Lamartine Yates,

1940, *61–2*). Astor and Rowntree believed there was no shortage of farmers' working capital but the problem was a shortage of fixed capital, which had been provided by the landlord before 1914 (Astor and Rowntree, 1938, *385*). The partial withdrawal of the upper class from landowning, and the financial problems of those remaining, led to less maintenance of farm buildings. The lack of landlord capital was important because owner-occupied farms accounted for only a third of farms in England and Wales in 1931, compared to 80 per cent in Europe (Sturmey, 1968, *299*; Kendall, 1941, *115*). The increased arable output of the wartime years had been achieved by capital consumption, and post-war depression allowed little opportunity to restore the fertility of this ploughed-up grassland. On the return to peace farmers often adapted their methods to make the best of their reduced circumstances and adopted capital-saving techniques. The increased livestock output in the interwar years was small, given the expansion in the area under permanent grass, and was achieved by allowing stock densities to fall. Milk recording studies showed that dairy farmers got a poor return from overfeeding low-yielding cows with expensive purchased foodstuffs. The worst examples of run-down land with choked drains, scrub-filled fields and dilapidated buildings were found in the marginal upland areas of Britain, although lower use of manures and lime was responsible for 'land-sickness' in some lowland districts and lime deficiency on upland pastures (Brown, 1989, *123*; Whetham, 1978, *192*, *196–7*; Astor and Rowntree, 1938, *135*, *137*, *141*, *209*). The farmers who did best were those who adopted enterprises with a relatively quick turnover which did not require excessive investment in elaborate farm buildings or expensive maintenance of marginal tillage land (Gavin, 1967, *194–5*; Keith, 1954, *42–4*, *51*, *60–8*; Mackie, 1992, *77–9*). Hence the popularity of milk, vegetables, eggs, poultry and pigs. There is no point in criticizing farmers for being rational and not employing capital they did not have, when it is unlikely that forgone output was of much value. Given the fact that prices were low and the land in question was marginal, the farmer who allowed it to return to rough pasture behaved in the same way as the industrialist who either shut down or mothballed part of his factory during the depression. If there was a loss it was only apparent after 1939, when depleted soil fertility increased the problems of reviving arable production once more.

Two types of farmers in particular were liable to find themselves forced to adopt land-extensive and low capital-intensity methods. The first were those farming heavy and intractable soils, such as the 'wheat and bean' lands of Essex, Huntingdon and other counties (Maxton (ed.), 1936, *124–7, 130–1*). These soils demanded expensive maintenance work on cultivation and fertilizers; until after 1945 and the advent of crawler tractors there was often little choice between rigid rotation of wheat, beans and fallow, and indifferent pasture. The high cost of cultivation and the fall in cereal prices squeezed out the working capital of many farmers in these districts; after a certain degree of neglect, the cost of reclamation, including perhaps heavy arrears of drainage work, outweighed any possible income to be derived from current prices. The other rigid structure was hill sheep farming, with output limited by climate, altitude and poor soil to wool and store stock. In the ten years after the First World War there was a brisk trade in breeding ewes while lowland flocks were rebuilt, but after 1930 these hill farms seldom provided more than a bare living for their operators (Grigg, 1989, *238–9*). Their slow-maturing cattle and three year-old-wethers became unpopular with consumers who preferred smaller joints from lowland lambs and baby beeves (Whetham, 1976, *24–7*). In Wales the wether flock (rams castrated to increase their meat-bearing capacity) practically disappeared, but the denser stocking of the hills with breeding ewes and their lambs led to further problems – an increased drain on the mineral content of the soil, the spread of bracken and an increase in disease (Whetham, 1978, *292*; Ashby and Evans, 1944, *170*). In many areas of Scotland even this limited adjustment was prohibited by the more severe climate, and there was a steady fall in the number of sheep and cattle maintained in the Highlands. The widely fluctuating but generally low prices obtained for the products of these areas in the last ten years before the Second World War thus intensified the deterioration in their farms and their low standards of housing and equipment (Whetham, 1952, *8*; Whetham, 1976, *25, 48–9, 52*; Maxton (ed.), 1936, *264–7*).

6
Tariff protection and other assistance

After the repeal of the Corn Production Act in August 1921 and the general lapse of wartime controls, the rest of the 1920s were a decade in which the government kept intervention to the barest minimum. The only remaining assistance to farmers in the 1920s was the continued derating of agricultural land and property, which had been in force since 1896, and the introduction of a subsidy for sugar beet in 1925.

Wartime inflation caused the average payment of local rates by farmers to rise from about 1s. 3d. an acre to around 3s. an acre. This was because rates were mainly determined by the level of rents and these increased sharply during the war. To ease this burden the 1923 Agricultural Rates Act halved the contribution of agricultural land to local rates. By a supplementary Act of 1925 farm buildings were derated, leaving farmers only having to pay rates on their dwelling houses. In 1927–8 rating allowances amounted to an average subsidy of £13 13s. per farmer in England and Wales. Obviously this relief was not large, and rates on the majority of farms represented less than 2 per cent of all outgoings. In 1929 the Agricultural Rates Act removed the remaining rates (amounting to £4,132,000) on agricultural land in England and Wales as part of a comprehensive scheme for relieving 'productive' industries. Similar relief from local rates was given to Scottish farmers but by a more involved method (Whetham, 1978, *161–2*; Venn, 1933, *194–9*). The subsidy on sugar beet might seem a strange aberration from the policy of non-assistance but the country's total dependence on imported supplies had been underlined by the experiences of the war and was seen as being undesirable. It was as an attempt to reduce this that a subsidy on sugar beet was instituted for the limited time of ten years under the British (Sugar) Subsidy Act of 1925. Small amounts of sugar beet had been grown in England since the 1870s and the first factory was opened in Suffolk in 1870. Attempts to establish a British sugar industry before 1910 had failed because of competition from cheaper traditional West Indian cane sugar and European beet sugar, the production of the latter established in the nineteenth century with government subsidies. By 1925 there was already a small industry in England supplying one factory established in 1912 by a Dutch firm at Cantley in Norfolk and another one in 1923 at Newark in Nottinghamshire, with a few thousand acres of beet each year. After the Subsidy Act the total acreage of sugar beet was recorded in the *Agricultural Returns* and rose to 349,000 acres in 1930 (MAFF, 1968, *102*), two thirds of this being in East Anglia where half of the eighteen factories in Britain were located. The other factories were in the west Midlands, Yorkshire, and one in Scotland at Cupar in Fife. It was not a major crop, and as yields were up to a third lower than in Europe, its expansion depended on the maintenance of the subsidy, but it provided a reasonable return for growers within 25 to 30 miles of a factory at a time when cereal prices were still falling (Astor and Murray, 1933, *xiii*; Grigg, 1989, *60*; Robinson, 1988, *186–91*; Astor and Rowntree, 1938, *95–8*).

In the 1930s British government assistance to farming came to exceed anything that had been offered before in peacetime, even in the early nineteenth century. At the same time as industrial depression and rising urban unemployment meant that domestic demand for agricultural produce remained low and failed to revive, worsening world depression meant that increasing quantities of low-priced food flooded into Britain. Following the election of October 1931, the newly formed National Government abruptly reversed Britain's long-established free trade policy to give more protection to industry, and in doing so ushered in an era of protection with imperial preference, and became a leading participant in tariff bargaining. The move towards protection was preceded by public discussion. Part of the debate was a study published under the title *Tariffs: The Case Examined* (1931). In this a panel of academic economists, under the chairmanship of Sir William Beveridge, presented the most coherent argument against all protection. The author of the chapter on agriculture, Lionel Robbins, argued that the case against protecting agriculture was even stronger than that against industrial protection. Higher incomes for farmers could only come out of the pockets of British consumers. Extra taxes on imported wheat would benefit both the Exchequer and agriculture, and encourage an expansion in the acreage of wheat, but leave the country as a whole worse off than the prevailing system of free trade (Robbins, 1931, *159–61*).

In the first place, the advantages of the territorial division of labour were particularly obvious and supported the proposition that the bulk of the world's wheat, and other agricultural commodities, should be produced in those countries where land was plentiful and natural conditions most suitable. Whatever there was to be said for British wheat growing it could not be said that it covered amounts of land to equal those of Canada and Argentina (Robbins, 1931, *157*). A detailed review of British agriculture revealed that its products differed materially in kind or quality from imported products that bore the same name, and were bought by different classes of consumers or were used for different purposes. In the case of British wheat this was a very different commodity from Canadian wheat. Whereas Canadian wheat was used for making bread, British wheat was mainly used in the manufacture of biscuits (Astor and Rowntree, 1938, *16*). Secondly – and unlike industry – there was no argument that protection was necessary while agriculture reorganized itself into larger or more rational production units (Robbins, 1931, *158*). Between 1870 and 1939 numbers of the smallest holdings of between 5 and 20 acres were in continuous decline, large farms of over 300 acres were in slight decline, whilst those in between with over 20 acres and fewer than 300 were increasing. Although the net effect of this was that the average size of farms hardly changed at all, there was no possibility that they could be amalgamated and enlarged to match the acreage, or emulate the style of management, found on North American prairie holdings (Astor and Rowntree, 1938, *369*; Grigg, 1989, *114*). Thirdly, as the numbers involved in British agriculture were small and the wages it paid were lower than those in industry, it was almost the last sector in which the government should intervene to create, or even to preserve jobs (Robbins, 1931, *158*). But although the net effect of protection made the urban worker worse off by raising the price of food, it should be remembered that at that time the prosperity of the urban worker depended much more on general demand factors affecting the levels of employment and wages than it did on any particular supply factors that influenced the cost of living (Lamartine Yates, 1940, *545*). Indeed, in the interwar years farm prices were themselves even more strongly determined by demand from the industrial sector than before 1914 (Capie, 1978, *51–3*).

The conclusions drawn by Beveridge's group had no influence on events, as their study appeared a few weeks before protection triumphed. In November 1931 the first emergency measure, the Abnormal Importation Act, was passed, imposing duties on a wide range of industrial products, and this was followed by the Horticultural Products Act (Emergency Customs Duties) in December 1931. The latter Act, which applied only to foreign imports of certain fruits and vegetables, was limited in duration to one year, and provided that the duties imposed should not exceed 100 per cent *ad valorem* (that is of the value of the imported product). The Act was due to expire on 11 December 1932, but the Orders made thereunder were terminated on 1 September 1932, and the duties were replaced by a new tariff imposed under the Import Duties Act, 1932. This measure, introduced on 1 March 1932, replaced the emergency measures with a general system of protection that lasted for the rest of the 1930s. It imposed a duty of 10 per cent *ad valorem* on all foreign imports, except those already dutiable and those specifically exempted by the Act. Among the free list were some agricultural products either produced in Britain or else used as inputs by British farmers. These were: wheat; livestock; meat; certain oilseeds (cottonseed, rapeseed, flaxseeds, soybeans); certain fruits; hides; skins; wool (Taylor and Taylor, 1943, *246–7*; Tracy, 1989, *150*).

In the event, protection of British agriculture could not take the same form as in the rest of Europe because substantial amounts of Empire agricultural products relied on the British market and so special preference had to be given to imperial goods. The majority of these were products that competed with British farmers and in 1929 Britain imported over £103 million worth of grain, meat, dairy products, and fruit from the Empire (Rooth, 1993, *76*). At the Imperial Economic Conference, held in Ottawa in the summer of 1932, the great staple food exports of the Dominions were granted preference, which meant their free entry to British markets, while quotas and tariffs were imposed on a range of agricultural goods from European and non-Empire countries. The British government made two main reservations in granting these concessions. Firstly, new duties on foreign wheat and some other products could be removed at any time if Empire supplies were inadequate. Secondly, the Dominions' expanding share of meat imports would not be allowed to interfere with the development of British production (Tracy, 1989, *150–1*). After the Ottawa agreements, concluded by Britain with Australia, New Zealand, Canada, Newfoundland, South Africa, Southern Rhodesia and British India, practically the only agricultural products with unrestricted entry into the United Kingdom were cotton, wool, hides and skins, and rubber (Taylor and Taylor, 1943, *247–8*).

The restrictions which applied to the importation of foreign agricultural products took different forms for different goods, the most frequent being the tariff preference. These preferences were widened in the case of numerous commodities such as dairy and poultry products, some fruits and certain vegetable oils, while their application to wheat and linseed was a new departure. Possible imports of foreign beef and mutton were limited to a quantity based on imports for the year July 1931–June 1932. While the Board of Trade Index of meat and fish prices rose in 1933 wholesale beef prices (a principal indicator) did not turn up before 1936–7. The sluggishness in prices led the British government to put forward in 1934 a long-term meat policy, though this only amounted to a general statement around which negotiations with overseas suppliers took place (Capie, 1978, *59*). Generally speaking, Empire products were to enter the United Kingdom freely but the Dominions undertook to limit frozen beef and mutton exports and, beginning with 1936, the United Kingdom could subject Empire dairy and poultry products to quotas or tariffs. The United Kingdom also reserved the right to regulate imports of Empire bacon and hams in connection with its Pigs and Bacon Marketing Schemes under which foreign bacon and hams were immediately limited as to volume. Among the most important to agriculture of the commercial treaties with foreign countries were those concluded in 1933 with Denmark, in 1933 and 1936 with Argentina and in 1938 with the United States (Taylor and Taylor, 1943, *248*). The volume of imports of agricultural products, which continued to rise until 1931, subsequently remained larger than in 1929 (Astor and Rowntree, 1938, *35–6*). The import-restricting effects of the depreciation of the pound were greatly weakened in the agricultural sector by the depreciation of the currencies in the Empire countries, Scandinavia and South America. Furthermore, as imports from the Empire were virtually unhindered by tariffs or quotas there were very few agricultural products in which a larger proportion of supplies did not come from imperial sources at the end of the decade than in 1931 (Rooth, 1993, *229–37*).

Beside the quantitative restrictions of tariffs and quotas on imports, aimed at reserving at least part of the domestic food market for the British farmer, the government introduced other forms of assistance which were intended to directly regulate the home market for the British producer under the Agricultural Marketing Acts of 1931 and 1933. The second of these also provided authority for import controls, although the 1931 Act was introduced by the Labour government which was not prepared to make any radical breach of free trade. At this time marketing reform at home seemed to offer an attractive alternative to protection. The 1931 Act allowed two-thirds of the producers in any branch of farming to adopt a marketing scheme with the approval of the Minister of Agriculture and Parliament; this then became binding on all producers. It could involve the enforcement of minimum and maximum prices and restrictions on the level of output, although the latter conflicted with any attempt to maintain employment in agriculture (Astor and Murray, 1933, *141–2*). The 1933 Act was passed by the protectionist National government which declared that if there was a satisfactory scheme for any product, it would regulate imports (Venn, 1933, *312–15*; Tracy, 1989, *152*).

Under these Acts there were eventually either subsidies or deficiency payments for beef, pork, butter, cheese, wheat, barley and oats. Milk and bacon had statutory marketing schemes as well as subsidies for milk. Hops also had a marketing scheme as well as a prohibition on new entrants. In addition, the sugar subsidy which had commenced in 1925, and was due to cease in 1934, was made permanent but the quantity of sugar eligible for support was limited (Astor and Rowntree, 1938, *438–9*). These additional internal methods of assistance were adopted because the import controls alone gave little protection for British agriculture. Even after Ottawa and the trade negotiations with foreign countries, Britain's farmers were still exposed to the full blast of competition from the Empire and most imports of agricultural products from foreign countries were subject only to relatively low duties. No government would consider measures that seriously undermined the traditional policy of cheap foodstuffs, especially in a time of acute depression (Tracy, 1989, *151–6*). Against this background market regulation schemes were seen as a relatively painless alternative to full tariff protection, for both government and consumers, while offering the appearance that something was being done to help the British farmer.

Some measures, like that applied to wheat, did give an extra stimulus to production. The market for this grain was not expanding and *per capita* consumption of wheat declined by 13 per cent in Britain between 1909–14 and 1934–9 (Collins, 1993, *23*). The 1932 Wheat Act guaranteed producers an average price of 10*s.* per cwt for millable wheat. But this was limited to a national output of up to 27 million cwt and the subsidy was proportionately reduced if this was exceeded. The payment was financed by a levy on flour, whether from home-produced or imported wheat. Market prices were well below the guaranteed level and the amount paid out in 1933–4 was £7.2 million. The Act stimulated a 52 per cent expansion of the wheat acreage between 1931 and 1935, largely at the expense of oats and barley which did not have subsidies until 1937, and each declined by a quarter of a million acres between 1931 and 1935. But the area devoted to wheat was never large and home production supplied only about a quarter of total requirements, which made the scheme workable. Wheat constituted only around 5 per cent of gross agricultural output and support was given almost for sentimental rather than economic reasons (Astor and Murray, 1933, *xi*; Astor and Rowntree, 1938, *82–5*; Maxton (ed.), 1936, *19–20*; Tracy, 1989, *152–3*).

Yet the Milk Marketing Board for England and Wales, set up at the end of 1933, could not pretend to be reserving even part of the domestic market for producers as there was no competition from imports. Instead its task was to bring order to a previously chaotic market. In the crisis of 1929–31 the large urban dairy companies who were the main milk buyers had gained the upper hand and forced down many producers' prices to unremunerative levels (Cohen, 1936, *ch. IV*). The Board succeeded in preventing this and ensured that a common price for milk was paid to all producers, both large and small, whether near to or distant from markets. It did this by operating as wholesaler and negotiating prices between producers and buyers of milk. The country was divided into eleven administrative regions and the regional boards arranged collection from producers and delivery to buyers. They also saw that contract prices for liquid sale and manufacturing milk were strictly observed, to prevent the previous practice of buying at lower manufacturing prices and then retailing the liquid milk (Cohen, 1936, *ch. V*; Brown, 1989, *120–2*). Of all the marketing schemes the Milk Marketing Board was the most comprehensive and successful, largely because it had control over producers to prevent the more efficient from undercutting the agreed prices. In Scotland the Marketing Board did not include the most northern parts of the country, and control over prices in the south was not as comprehensive as in England. The Scots farmer far from a market got even less for his milk than his English counterpart, though where they operated the Scottish milk boards did offer the distant producer at least some protection in the 1930s (Mackie, 1992, *78–9*; Astor and Rowntree, 1938, *279–80*).

The marketing schemes do illustrate one area where the British farmer was thought to have had less in common with the European farmer, and that was the question of cooperation (Mackie, 1992, *570–2*; Astor and Murray, 1933, *63, 85–101*). In Denmark in 1937, 85 per cent of bacon output was handled by 62 cooperative bacon factories, but Britain had only six in 1923 (Lamartine Yates, 1940, *48*; Whetham, 1978, *151*). In the 1930s British bacon factories found their expansion held back because they had difficulty in obtaining sufficient throughput (Astor and Rowntree, 1938, *223–4*). Farmers' cooperative societies, though not as universal or successful as in Denmark, were more common in Europe for production, processing and marketing than they were in Britain (Lamartine Yates, 1940, *114, 150, 304–6, 354–5, 432–3*). In this country enthusiasts established a variety of institutions to advise and encourage cooperative societies, but in general little change was achieved in the face of the apathy of most farmers. There were a number of societies formed during the First World War but the immediate post-war and 1929–32 depressions took a heavy toll of these. They were most successful in areas where small farmers followed a similar pattern of production – cheese factories in Leicestershire and north Wales, milk collection centres in Derbyshire and the Dorset vales, and horticultural sales and distribution societies in Worcestershire (Whetham, 1978, *28, 152*). In Wales the first 'boom' in the establishment of produce societies was largely due to the encouragement officially given to the making of cheese during the First World War, but they were badly hit by the heavy fall in the price of cheese which began in 1921 and their numbers soon began to decline. The last of the cheese societies ceased in 1936 and by 1939 Wales had only eight produce societies, six of which were dairy societies heavily committed to the sale of butter and milk. Welsh societies devoted to the purchase and distribution of agricultural requisites like fertilizers and feeding stuffs had a greater success and although their number fell from 83 in 1920 to 53 in 1939 their membership rose from 21,000 to 26,000 (Ashby and Evans, 1944, *116–24*). But the failure of cooperative societies to reach more than a fraction of farmers may not have indicated either excessive individualism or lack of enterprise; it could merely signal the fact that the nature of British farm production was unsuited to this form of organization.

Of the three methods of assistance – tariffs, deficiency payments, and market regulation – the first was of little practical help as tariffs and quotas were seriously weakened by imperial preferences and concessions to individual trading partners. The major impact of government help to the agricultural sector came through deficiency payments and marketing schemes (Brown, 1991, *187*). The value of all relief measures taken together – grants and subsidies; relief from taxation in various forms; and indirect forms of assistance like preferential rail rates and tithe legislation – was estimated to have an annual value to agriculture of £45 million in 1933 (Astor and Murray, 1933, *17*). Under these the volume of agricultural production in Great Britain increased by more than one-sixth between 1930–1 and 1936–7, but prices remained low (Taylor and Taylor, 1943, *249*). In 1933 the index of agricultural prices

(1927–9 = 100) reached its lowest point at 76. Prices rose thereafter but even at their highest point in the later 1930s they only stood at 89. If the subsidies on wheat, cattle and milk are taken into account they made a slight difference, raising the general index to 77 in 1933 and 91 in 1937 (Tracy, 1989, *159*). But dependence on imports remained very great, their volume was reduced from the high crisis levels of 1931 but there was little overall change in their volume between 1927–9 and 1936–8. Prior to the outbreak of war in September 1939 it was estimated that Britain was dependent upon overseas sources for 60–65 per cent of her food requirements. Imports furnished rather more than half the meat supplies, about 70 per cent of the cheese and sugar supplies, and around 90 per cent of the cereals and fat supplies. It is therefore not surprising that tariffs and quotas were so limited. Their main effect was a shift in the pattern of food imports away from foreign countries in favour of the Empire. In 1929 its share had not yet reached 37 per cent, but in 1937 the Empire was furnishing more than half the agricultural products imported into the United Kingdom (Taylor and Taylor, 1943, *249*; Tracy, 1989, *161*).

7

The structure of rural society

After 1850 there was a decline in the importance of the rural population and a reduction in the size of the agricultural labour force. Precise measurement of the former is not possible because it is hard to say where towns and suburbs shade off into the countryside. But we do know from the Census that the total agricultural labour force, which includes farmers and farmworkers, fell from around 2 million in 1851 to about 1.3 million in 1931. The rural population and the farm workforce are not synonymous because the former included a significant number who were in non-farming occupations. Most supplied and serviced the farming community and they included village blacksmiths, shoemakers, potters, shopkeepers, and innkeepers, as well as smaller numbers who provided professional services such as clerics, schoolteachers, auctioneers, lawyers and land agents. Some of those in occupations allied to farming had small amounts of land and combined farming with their main occupation (Grigg, 1989, *138*). This could include butchers and livestock dealers with accommodation land, and village shopkeepers and publicans with a smallholding, but they would only be recorded in the Census under their main job. The agricultural labour force fell in the face of farmers' increased pressure to mechanize and the fact that urban life offered higher wages and a more attractive style of living than could be obtained in the countryside. As the number of farmworkers declined they needed fewer of the village services. We do not know exactly what happened to the numbers of rural shopkeepers, but there was certainly a decline in the number of rural fairs and markets supplying those requirements from their pre-1870 highpoint (Mingay (ed.), 1981, 1, *304–8*).

Rural crafts and industries were also subject to pressures that were independent of the declining numbers in farming. Some, like milling, moved from the countryside to the town as home supplies of grain shrank in the face of growing quantities of imports that were processed at the ports. The improved transport network meant the output of town factories could be sent quickly and cheaply to country districts (Horn, 1984a, *138–50*). The ready availability of cheap manufactured goods destroyed many of the older rural industries after 1870. Factory production and foreign competition combined to ruin the underwood trades; the makers of baskets, besoms, barrel-hoops and all manner of coppice-ware had largely disappeared by 1914. As the slate industry and tile manufacture grew, the need for skilled thatchers diminished, while galvanized sheeting was now used on the roofs of farm buildings. The number of thatchers declined from 4140 in 1871 to 3210 in 1891. Even those trades directly servicing agriculture were affected. The mechanization of the corn harvest soon extinguished the scythe-handler and the rake-maker, and the disappearance of the arable flock and sheepfold had the same effect upon the hurdle-maker (Horn, 1984b, *138–9*; Creasey and Ward, 1984, *12*). But not all rural crafts declined in this era. Between 1871 and 1901 the numbers of blacksmiths, straw product manufacturers (including hat-makers), thatchers, coopers, and millwrights all fell but there was an increase in the numbers of saddle- and harness-makers, carpenters, joiners, and boot and shoe makers (Mingay (ed.), 1981, 1, *316*). Some survived by adapting their businesses to the new technology; village blacksmiths ceased to make farm implements themselves but acted as agents and did servicing for factory-produced farm machinery (Horn, 1984b, *141*).

Within the market town, as distinct from the village, industry had greater protection from the misfortunes of agriculture. As food processing became increasingly factory-based, partly at the expense of farmhouse production, such activities as bacon-curing, cheese and butter making were shifted to factories in market towns like Calne, Chippenham, and Devizes in Wiltshire, Melton Mowbray in Leicestershire, Middlewich in Cheshire, and Staverton in Devon. Other industries that prospered up to 1914 were branches of agricultural engineering where, even if the home market was stagnant in some years, firms like Ransomes in Ipswich and Paxmans at Colchester could find a sale for steam and gas engines and threshing machines overseas (Brown, 1986, *83–5, 90–1*).

The economic pressures on the structure of rural society were intensified after 1918. Continued decline of the population made further inroads on the precarious balance between farming and its servicing trades, and the fall in numbers of farmworkers was accompanied by complaints of their declining quality as well (Street, 1932, *265*). By 1939 the larger village manufacturers had practically vanished, leaving only a small number of ageing craftsmen who were too old to learn new skills and were condemned to lead a solitary and impoverished existence. The future of the wheelwright, blacksmith, saddle- and harness-maker was secure only as long as the horse was the predominant source of draught power on the farm. By the 1930s this supremacy was challenged (Collins, 1983, *94*) and also by then the contraction of arable acreage had hit small engineering workshops and even the business of the larger implement makers by reducing the demand for cultivating and harvesting equipment. Rural brickworks found less demand for drainage tiles as underdraining was not maintained, while at the same time cheaper factory-made bricks reduced the building supply side of their trade (Creasey and Ward, 1984, *13*). The impact of this final decline of the village tradesman on rural social structure was greater than the numbers involved might suggest. In Victorian times the craftsman was more likely to be an incomer to the parish than the farmworker and as such was more likely to bring fresh ideas and opinions (Horn, 1984b, *141–2*). In the interwar years the village came to be dominated by the interests of workers and farmers and, deprived of both the socially enlivening influence of the tradesmen as well as the convenience of locally provided services, it became an increasingly unattractive place to live.

Further reductions in the size of the farm labour force were an obvious feature of the interwar years (Armstrong, 1988, *174*). The regular full-time workers of both sexes in England and Wales declined from 685,000 in 1921 to 630,000 in 1930 and to 511,000 in 1939. The contraction was only 8 per cent in the 1920s but more severe in the 1930s when it plummeted by 19 per cent. The drift from farm work was greatest where alternative employment was easiest to find. It was for this reason that the greatest losses were in the midland and southern counties in England where the new and expanding consumer goods industries were to be found, and the least in the northern counties where depressed heavy industries like coal-mining and ship-building were also losing labour (Astor and Rowntree, 1938, *308*; Armstrong, 1988, *175–6*). Scotland, which depended even more upon heavy industry than England, experienced a lower decline. It had 104,000 regular full-time agricultural workers in 1921, falling by only 5 per cent in the 1920s to 99,000 in 1930. As in England, the loss increased in the 1930s but only to 9 per cent so that there were still 90,000 full-time Scottish farmworkers in 1939 (MAFF, 1968, *62*). In all parts of Britain there were also a number of part-time workers, as there had been before 1914. They were either the members of farming families or else the casuals who were called upon at harvest. The introduction of the milking machine and the continued decline of the farmhouse cheese and butter industries reduced the employment of farm women (Whetham, 1978, *208–9, 236*). In addition, the continued decline in the acreage of all arable crops and the increased mechanization of harvesting reduced the amount of seasonal work (Astor and Rowntree, 1938, *311*). As a result the number of part-time workers declined much more rapidly than those employed full-time, from 207,000 in 1921 to 110,000 in 1939, a loss of 47 per cent (MAFF, 1968, *62*).

Throughout the whole period from 1870 to 1940 the function of a vigorous rural society as a foundation for industrial society was continuously debated. Many were gravely concerned at the rapid change which was coming over the countryside and more especially by the flight of labour from the land. Moved more perhaps by sentiment than by a dispassionate analysis of current economic and social trends in the industry itself, a considerable body of opinion in this, as in many continental countries, advocated the establishment of smallholdings as a sovereign cure for all the ills to which the agricultural flesh was heir (Pratt, 1906). This remedy was not the prerogative of any particular political party, though it may seem strange that slogans such as 'Back to the Land' and 'Three Acres and a Cow' should have made a particular appeal to some advocates of international free trade.

Be that as it may, the creation of smallholdings was the first essay at a constructive agricultural policy adopted in modern times even though it was largely inspired by highly coloured visions of an imaginary past (Ashby and Evans, 1944, *128*). But the advocates of this argument had diminishing force after 1890. The interwar years experienced a continued exodus of labour from the countryside, at an even faster rate in the 1930s than in the 1920s, in response to low earnings and poor rural amenities (Armstrong, 1988, *200–1*). It was recognized that attempts to create a class of independent peasant cultivators were anachronistic and that Britain differed from Europe in this respect. The interwar years also saw the land-owning classes reduce their role in rural society, and no other social group filled their place. This was a further factor in the decline of the rural economy as the knock-on effects of landlord spending provided both work and services for a significant number of rural dwellers before 1914. The loss of jobs in estate yards, home farms and woodlands affected males whilst the closing of mansions and country houses reduced the employment of females in domestic service. The allegation that there was a haemorrhage of the most talented into other occupations that provided a better standard of living was applied not only to farm and other workers but to the farmers themselves (Astor and Rowntree, 1938, *371–2*).

The feature most likely to retain labour on the land was the small farm, or smallholding of the type to be found in Europe. But economic facts provided no support for this institution and neither did people's personal preferences. Most farms of fewer than 100 to 150 acres were inefficient, and although income per acre may have been high, they were too small and lacking in capital to provide anything other than a very low income and poor standard of living for their occupants. Efforts by middle-class idealists between 1880 and 1914 to entice former town dwellers back to a 'better' style of life on the land in a variety of agrarian communes, cottage farms and farm colonies did not attract more than a few dozen persons (Marsh, 1982, *93–135*). Some nineteenth-century landowners added to this by the establishment of smallholdings on their own estates. These had a similar limited amount of success, as well as attracting opposition from local farmers who argued that they diminished their supplies of labour (Ernle, 1912, *31*). In spite of such discouragements, official efforts were also made at times to create more of these farms. The 1892 Small Holdings Act and the

1908 Smallholdings and Allotments Act empowered county councils to purchase agricultural land to lease as smallholdings. Between 1908 and 1914 some 200,000 acres were acquired by county councils and some 14,000 holdings were created. Many of these holdings were just bare land and were let to families who already had houses and buildings; only 886 new houses were built. The failure of all these efforts was made clear by the fact the numbers of small farms under 50 acres showed no perceptible increase (Orwin and Whetham, 1964, *331–5*; Grigg, 1989, *119*). The movement continued after the First War with the 1919 Land Settlement (Facilities) Act which was designed to meet the government's promise to provide a smallholding for any returning ex-serviceman who wanted one. About 250,000 acres were bought by county councils for this purpose and settled by 17,000 tenants. By 1925 this measure, and the pre-war legislation, had given the county councils 438,000 acres with nearly 30,000 tenants. Between 1926 and 1932 another 30,000 acres were bought and a further 1270 holdings provided. But the rents obtained on these holdings hardly paid 3 per cent on the capital borrowed by the county councils to set them up, so ratepayers and taxpayers provided a considerable subsidy to their occupiers (Whetham, 1978, *137–9, 217*). Their small size often made them an agricultural dead-end, unable to generate sufficient profits to allow landless men without money to build up enough capital either to purchase their own small farms or else to become tenants of larger farms.

8

Conclusion

The 70 years from 1870 to 1940 were predominantly a 'down' period for British agriculture during which prices, profits and confidence were low. Although there was moderate improvement in the 10 years or so before the First World War, and higher profits were experienced from 1916 to 1921, this was not long enough to counteract the long-term influences preventing agriculture from attaining any solid prosperity. International competition in the principal items of farm produce set the downward spiral in motion in the late 1870s, and this placed even greater pressure on British farming in the late 1920s and 1930s.

The picture to emerge is that there were two agricultural depressions in this period (Ojala, 1952, *208–9*). The first, beginning in the 1880s and lasting till 1896, was far less severe than the second, that encompassed the span of years from 1924 to 1940. In the pre-1896 depression the real value of British gross agricultural output did not decline but fluctuated around a stationary trend, and slightly rose after this date (Turner, 1992). This was because the growth of world supply of agricultural products was more than matched by the increase in world demand. Before the First World War the international economy was free from major shocks and depressions. Industry, employment and trade grew steadily, thereby generating sufficient increase in purchasing power to absorb the growing volume of low-priced agricultural goods. The important change for British farmers was being able to take advantage of the growing prosperity of British consumers and to continue to switch their emphasis away from relatively cheap cereals into the dearer livestock sector (Collins and Jones, 1967; Fletcher, 1961a). Although there were rigidities in the system and costs involved in this process, they were not able to hamper this broad transformation of the sector enough to prevent it from maintaining the value of its output (Thompson, 1991).

In the depressions after 1920 both arable and livestock sectors experienced reversals and between 1911–13 and 1935–9 the real values of each output in Britain fell by 17 and 16 per cent, respectively (Ojala, 1952, *209*). The revisionist view of the British economy at large is that generally there was considerable growth throughout the interwar years, and although there was a severe downturn after 1929, recover dates from the middle of 1932. Although by some definitions this may be true, agriculture was one of the sectors that showed little sign of recovery (Capie, 1978, *51–2*). The root of its problems in the 1930s lay in the persistently depressed international economy. In 1931–7 the average volume of world non-agricultural exports was 25 per cent below the level for 1929, while the average volume of agricultural exports was only 8 per cent below (Taylor and Taylor, 1943, *6*). Before 1914 Britain paid for a substantial portion of food imports with exports of industrial goods and services. In the 1930s depressed exports and high industrial unemployment in Britain and the world resulted in stagnant demand and low prices for all agricultural products. Since 1870 government had left the industry unprotected from the full impact of market forces, so British farmers shared the experience of low world prices. It did intervene from 1930 onwards but as the measures taken were restricted and selective the market prices of most important foodstuffs remained low. After 1870 farming became too small a part of the national economy to carry much weight against budgetary and industrial considerations (Brown, 1991).

However, these years did not see uniform depression for all sectors of agriculture. Livestock-producing regions, with a brief interruption in the First World War, fared relatively better than corn-growing ones and some others were able to develop profitable enterprises in market gardening and other areas. Technical change was necessary, and although scope for some forms of mechanization was still limited before 1940, those farmers who by efficient management were able to obtain a high return from capital and labour were the most successful. One feature present in all regions was an even greater specialization after 1870 (Robinson, 1988).

This can be seen in the case of Wales. Wales was not really suited to wheat production and the Welsh farmer found it more profitable to purchase imported flour than to produce the corn himself. The wheat area of the Principality fell from 148,000 acres in 1870 to a mere 13,000 in 1939. But driven by rising real incomes and increased demand for livestock products the cattle population of Wales rose by a third from 645,000 in 1870 to 859,000 in 1939, while sheep increased by over 60 per cent from 2,902,000 in 1870 to 4,648,000 during the same period. Although not easily measured in quantitative terms, there was an improvement in the quality of the livestock carried. There was also a change in the nature of demand for livestock products. Welsh flockmasters turned their attention from the production of mutton to lamb, while graziers devoted more attention to producing younger beef instead of the three-year-old runts of earlier days. In both these directions the Welsh farmer was still exposed, though in varying measures, to competition from overseas. This was particularly true of butter and cheese, which had once been associated with stock rearing. The Welsh farmer, as did others, withdrew from this area and concentrated increasingly on the market for liquid milk. By 1939 at least half the farmers of Wales had turned their attention to this relatively new branch of the industry (Ashby and Evans, 1944, *167–8*). These developments were mirrored, with appropriate local variations, in other parts of the country. The long-term decline in farmhouse cheese and butter making and concentration on milk meant that farmers withdrew from this aspect of food processing and simply became producers. Some market garden and vegetable products were marketed by their growers in 1870, but railways, the appearance of a network of wholesalers, and the development of motor transport after 1920 made this a rarity. Sheep and cattle feeders in 1870 grew a substantial proportional amount of fodder crops, but the increase of pasture at the expense of tillage and the use of cheap artificial feedstuffs rendered this redundant. Between 1850 and 1880 – the High Farming period – mixed farming reached its apogee (Jones, 1962; Thompson, 1968). But from the 1870s to 1940 the system was steadily undermined by the decline in agricultural prices: its final demise came about after 1950 when the advance of chemical and mechanical technology rendered its principles obsolete (Grigg, 1989, *181*).

Bibliography

Official publications

Report of the Royal Commission on the Depressed Condition of the Agricultural Interests, PP (1881), xv, xvii; (1882), xiv.

Report of the Royal Commission on Agricultural Depression, PP (1894), xvi; (1895), xvi, xvii; (1896), xvi; (1897), xv.

Interim Report of the Royal Commission on Agriculture, PP (1919), viii.

Report of the Board of Agriculture and Fisheries on Wages and Conditions of Employment in Agriculture, PP (1919), ix.

Ministry of Agriculture, Fisheries and Food (MAFF) (1968) *A Century of Agricultural Statistics: Great Britain 1866–1966* (London).

General studies

Bellerby, J. R. (1956) *Agriculture and Industry Relative Income* (London).

Bellerby, J. R. (1968) 'The distribution of farm income in the United Kingdom, 1867–1938', reprinted in W. E. Minchinton (ed.), *Essays in Agrarian History*, vol. II (Newton Abbot), pp. 259–78.

Brown, J. (1989) *Agriculture in England: A Survey of Farming, 1870–1947* (Manchester). How farmers survived by introducing new products and using new techniques, comparing failures and success stories.

Brown, J. (1991) 'The state and agriculture, 1914–72', in G. Jones and M. Kirby (eds), *Competitiveness and the State: Government and Business in Twentieth Century Britain* (Manchester), pp. 181–98.

Cohen, R. L. (1936) *The History of Milk Prices* (Oxford). An analysis of the factors that affected milk and dairy product prices before and after 1914, including the marketing scheme of the 1930s.

Collins, E. J. T. (1983) 'The farm horse economy of England and Wales in the early tractor age 1900–40', in F. M. L. Thompson (ed.), *Horses in European Economic History* (Reading), pp. 73–99.

Collins, E. J. T. (1993) 'Why wheat? Choice of food grains in Europe in the nineteenth and twentieth centuries', *Journal of European Economic History*, 22, 1, 7–38.

Crafts, N. F. R. (1985) *British Economic Growth During the Industrial Revolution* (Oxford).

Feinstein, C. H. (1972) *National Income, Expenditure and Output of the United Kingdom, 1855–1965* (Cambridge).

Grigg, D. (1989) *English Agriculture: An Historical Perspective* (Oxford). A clear introduction to the establishment and evolution of farming patterns in England (and Wales) from the seventeenth century to the present.

Kindleberger, C. P. (1964) *Economic Growth in France and Britain 1851–1950* (Cambridge, Massachusetts). Presents a novel interpretation of the failure of British agriculture to transform in response to the low prices after 1880.

Layton, W. T. (1920) *An Introduction to the Study of Prices* (London).

Murray, K. A. H. (1931) *Factors Affecting the Price of Livestock in Great Britain* (Oxford). Covers the period from 1870 to 1929.

Ojala, E. M. (1952) *Agriculture and Economic Progress* (Oxford). This work provided the initial estimates of British agricultural output, used by Fletcher (1961a), and subsequent writers.

Orwin, C. S. and Whetham, E. H. (1964) *A History of British Agriculture 1846–1914* (London). Provides a general coverage of both the period of high farming and depression in the 1880s and 1890s.

Sturmey, S. G. (1968) 'Owner-farming in England and Wales, 1900–1950', reprinted in W. E. Minchinton (ed.), *Essays in Agrarian History*, Vol. II (Newton Abbot) pp. 283–306.

Taylor, D. (1976) 'The English dairy industry, 1860–1930', *Economic History Review*, 2nd ser., XXIX, 4, 585–601.

Taylor, D. (1987) 'Growth and structural change in the English dairy industry, c.1860–1930', *Agricultural History Review*, 35, I, 47–64.

Taylor, F. D. W. (1955) 'United Kingdom: numbers in agriculture', *Farm Economist*, VII, 4, 36–40.

Tracy, M. (1989) *Government and Agriculture in Western Europe 1880–1988*, 3rd edn (London). Earlier editions published under the titles: *Agriculture in Western Europe: Crisis and Adaptation since 1880* (1964); *Agriculture in Western Europe: Challenge and Response 1880–1980* (1982). An important study comparing UK reaction to depression in the 1880s and 1930s with that of France, Germany and Denmark.

High farming before 1880

Chambers, J. D. and Mingay, G. E. (1966) *The Agricultural Revolution 1750–1880* (London).

Collins, E. J. T. and Jones, E. L. (1967) 'Sectoral advance in English agriculture, 1850–80', *Agricultural History Review*, xv, II, 65–81. Refutes Sturgess's (1966) 'revolution' on the English clays, arguing there was merely a series of unsatisfactory adaptations to the swings of the market towards livestock production.

Jones, E. L. (1962) 'The changing basis of agricultural prosperity, 1853–1873', *Agricultural History Review*, x, II, 102–19.

Phillips, A. D. M. (1969) 'Underdraining in the English claylands, 1850–80: a review', *Agricultural History Review*, 17, I, 44–55. A contribution to the debate in Collins and Jones (1967), Sturgess (1966), and Thompson (1968) which argues that underdrainage could be a worthwhile component of agricultural investment, a view reiterated in Phillips (1989).

Phillips, A. D. M. (1989) *The Underdraining of Farmland in England During the Nineteenth Century* (Oxford).

Sturgess, R. W. (1966) 'The agricultural revolution on the English clays', *Agricultural History Review*, xiv, II, 104–21. This article, arguing that high farming techniques significantly increased clayland productivity provoked a debate with Collins and Jones (1967).

Sturgess, R. W. (1967) 'The agricultural revolution on the English clays: a rejoinder', *Agricultural History Review*, xv, II, 82–7.

Thompson, F. M. L. (1968) 'The second agricultural revolution, 1815–1880', *Economic History Review*, 2nd ser., xxi, 1, 62–77. An important pioneering article that made the first attempts to quantify the inputs into British farming during the era of high farming.

Wilmot, S. (1990) '*The Business of Improvement': Agriculture and Scientific Culture in Britain c. 1700–c.1870* (Bristol). Comes to the conclusion that the real effects of the application of science to British agriculture were very limited.

Depression in the 1880s and 1890s

Atkins, P. J. (1977–8) 'The growth of London's railway milk trade, c.1845–1914', *Journal of Transport History*, n.s., 4, 208–26.

Channing, F. A. (1897) *The Truth About Agricultural Depression* (London). The author was a member of the 1894–97 Royal Commission on Agricultural Depression and presents a selection taken from the evidence given before it.

Ernle, Lord (1912) *English Farming Past and Present* (London). Reprinted in 1961 (6th edn) with an introduction by G. E. Fussell and O. R. McGregor. His picture of universal depression provides the focus for most post-war studies of British agriculture on the period 1870–1914.

Fisher, J. R. (1975) *Clare Sewell Read 1826–1905. A Farmers' Spokesman of*

the Late Nineteenth Century (Hull). A portrait of the only tenant
farmer in the House of Commons in the nineteenth century.

Fletcher, T. W. (1961a) 'The Great Depression in English agriculture,
1873–96', *Economic History Review*, 2nd ser., XIII, 417–32. The
path-breaking revisionist article that challenged Lord Ernle's as-
sumption of general agricultural depression after 1870.

Fletcher, T. W. (1961b) 'Lancashire livestock farming during the Great
Depression', *Agricultural History Review*, IX, I, 17–42.

Harley, C. K. (1992) 'The world food economy and pre-World War I
Argentina', in S. N. Broadberry and N. F. R. Crafts (eds),
Britain in the International Economy 1870–1914 (Cambridge), pp.
244–68.

Jones, E. L. (1964) *Seasons and Prices: The Role of the Weather in English
Agricultural History* (London). Contains graphic accounts of the
bad weather and poor harvests of the late 1870s and early 1880s.

Ó Gráda, C. (1979) 'The landlord and agricultural transformation, 1870–
1900: a comment on Richard Perren's hypothesis', *Agricultural
History Review*, 27, I, 40–2.

Ó Gráda, C. (1981) 'Agricultural decline 1860–1914', in R. Floud and D.
McCloskey (eds), *The Economic History of Britain Since the 1700s*,
vol. 2: *1860 to the 1970s* (Cambridge), pp. 175–97. Compares
changes in the incomes of landowners, tenants and workers, as well
as the likely impact of a tariff on imported corn.

Olson, M. and Harris, C. C. (1959) ' "Free trade in corn": a statistical
study of the prices and production of wheat in Great Britain from
1873 to 1896', *Quarterly Journal of Economics*, 73, 145–68.

Perren, R. (1970) 'The landlord and agricultural transformation 1870–
1900', *Agricultural History Review*, 18, I, 36–51. Argues that investment by landlords in livestock areas was sometimes able to stem
rent reductions, disputed by Ó Gráda (1979) above.

Perren, R. (1978) *The Meat Trade in Britain, 1870–1914* (London).

Perren, R. (1979) 'The landlord and agricultural transformation, 1870–
1914: a rejoinder', *Agricultural History Review*, 27, I, 43–6. A reply
to Ó Gráda (1979) above.

Perry, P. J. (1972) 'Where was the "Great Agricultural Depression"?': a
geography of agricultural bankruptcy in late Victorian England and
Wales', *Agricultural History Review*, 20, I, 30–45. Uses statistics of
bankruptcies among farmers to present a regional picture of the
depression.

Perry, P. J. (1974) *British Farming in the Great Depression, 1870–1914: An
Historical Geography* (1974). Argues that Fletcher's (1961a) distinc-
tion between prosperous livestock and depressed corn farmers is an
oversimplification.

Perry, P. J. (ed.) (1973) *British Agriculture 1875–1914* (London). Contains reprints of a number of articles including Fletcher (1961a & b), Olsen and Harris (1959), Perren (1970) and Perry (1972).

Thompson, F. M. L. (1991) 'The anatomy of English agriculture, 1870–1914', in B. A. Holderness and M. Turner (eds), *Land, Labour and Agriculture, 1700–1920* (London), pp. 210–40.

Turner, M. E. (1992) 'Output and prices in UK agriculture, 1867–1914, and the Great Agricultural Depression reconsidered', *Agricultural History Review*, 40, I, 38–51. Argues that grain output decreased from the late 1860s, well before the dramatic fall in corn prices after 1879.

Whetham, E. H. (1964) 'The London milk trade, 1860–1900', *Economic History Review*, 2nd ser., xvi, 369–80. A survey of the factors that stimulated its long-distance transport by rail.

The First World War

Armstrong, W. A. (1991) 'Kentish rural society during the First World War', in B. A. Holderness and M. Turner (eds), *Land, Labour and Agriculture, 1700–1920* (London), pp. 109–31.

Dewey, P. E. (1975) 'Agricultural labour supply in England and Wales during the First World War', *Economic History Review*, 2nd ser., xxviii, 1, 100–12.

Dewey, P. E. (1979) 'Government provision of farm labour in England and Wales during the First World War', *Agricultural History Review*, 27, II, 110–21.

Dewey, P. E. (1984) 'British farming profits and government policy during the First World War', *Economic History Review*, 2nd ser., xxxvii, 3, 373–90.

Dewey, P. E. (1989) *British Agriculture in the First World War* (London).

Dewey, P. E. (1991) 'Production problems in British agriculture during the First World War', in B. A. Holderness and M. Turner (eds), *Land, Labour and Agriculture, 1700–1920* (London), pp. 241–54.

Horn, P. (1984a) *Rural Life in England during the First World War* (Dublin). A well-documented survey of social conditions.

Middleton, T. H. (1923) *Food Production in War* (Oxford).

Offer, A. (1989) *The First World War: An Agrarian Interpretation* (Oxford).

The interwar depression

Astor, Viscount and Murray, K. A. H. (1933) *The Planning of Agriculture* (Oxford). Critical of most features of government assistance to agriculture in the 1929–32 depression.

Astor, Viscount and Rowntree, B. S. (1938) *British Agriculture: The Principles of Future Policy* (London). An important critical study of British farming in the interwar years.

Capie, F. (1978) 'Australian and New Zealand Competition in the British Market', *Australian Economic History Review*, XVIII, 1, 46–63.

Cooper, A. F. (1986) 'Another look at the "Great Betrayal"', *Agricultural History*, 60, 3, 80–104. Partly revises the picture presented in Taylor and Taylor (1943) and Whetham (1978), pp. 139–41.

Cooper, A. F. (1989) *British Agricultural Policy, 1912–1936: A Study in Conservative Politics* (Manchester).

Creasey, J. S. and Ward, S. B. (1984) *The Countryside Between the Wars 1918–1940* (London). A detailed photographic account of British farming and related activities between 1919 and 1939.

Kendall, M. J. (1941) 'The Financing of British Agriculture', *Journal of the Royal Statistical Society*, CIV, II, 111–42.

Lamartine Yates, P. (1940) *Food Production in Western Europe: An Economic Survey of Agriculture in Six Countries* (London). An analysis of the successful competition from some continental farmers for parts of the British food market.

Orr, J. B. (1938) *Food Health and Income* (London).

Robbins, L. (1931) 'The Case of Agriculture', in W. H. Beveridge *et al., Tariffs: The Case Examined* (London), pp. 148–69.

Rooth, T. (1993) *British Protectionism and the International Economy: Overseas Commercial Policy in the 1930s* (Cambridge). Chapters 3 and 8 cover imperial preference, the Ottawa Conference, and agricultural policy and imports.

Taylor, H. C. and Taylor, A. D. (1943) *World Trade in Agricultural Products* (New York). Surveys the situation from 1924 to 1939 with particular emphasis on the problems of the 1930s.

Venn, J. A. (1933) *Foundations of Agricultural Economics*, 2nd edition (London).

Whetham, E. H. (1952) *British Farming, 1939–1949* (London). The first two chapters summarize the rundown state of farming in the interwar years and the situation in 1939.

Whetham, E. H. (1974) 'The Agriculture Act 1920 and its repeal – the "Great Betrayal"', *Agricultural History Review*, 22, I, 36–49. Uses oral history interviews with farmers who remembered this event.

Whetham, E. H. (1976) *Beef Cattle and Sheep 1910–1940* (Cambridge).

Whetham, E. H. (1978) *The Agrarian History of England and Wales*: vol. VIII, *1914–1939* (Cambridge).

Rural society

Armstrong, A. (1988) *Farmworkers: A Social and Economic History 1770–1980* (London). Chapters 5–8 provide an excellent general survey of all aspects of the British farmworker's life.

Brown, J. (1986) *The English Market Town: A Social and Economic History 1750–1914* (Marlborough).

Campbell, R. H. (1991) *Owners and Occupiers: Changes in Rural Society in South-West Scotland before 1914* (Aberdeen).

Dunbabin, J. P. D. (1968) 'The incidence and organisation of agricultural trades unionism in the 1870s', *Agricultural History Review*, 16, II, 114–41.

Dunbabin, J. P. D. (1974) *Rural Discontent in Nineteenth Century Britain* (London). Deals mainly with agricultural labour but also contains a chapter on tenant right.

Horn, P. (1984b) *The Changing Countryside in Victorian and Edwardian England and Wales* (London).

Marsh, J. (1982) *Back to the Land: the Pastoral Impulse in Victorian England from 1880 to 1914* (London).

Mingay, G. E. (ed.) (1981) *The Victorian Countryside*, 2 vols (London). A survey containing 46 articles covering many aspects of life in the Victorian countryside and country town, together with 172, mainly photographic, illustrations.

Thompson, F. M. L. (1963) *English Landed Society in the Nineteenth Century* (London). Covers all aspects of aristocratic life, including long-term decline from 1830 to 1939 (pp. 269–345).

Regional studies

Ashby, A. W. and Evans, I. L. (1944) *The Agriculture of Wales and Monmouth* (Cardiff). Surveys the main features of Welsh agriculture with special emphasis on the 1930s.

Howell, D. W. (1977) *Land and People in Nineteenth Century Wales* (London).

Maxton, J. P. (ed.) (1936) *Regional Types of British Agriculture* (London). Chapters by fifteen authors, covering all regions.

Perren, R. (1989) 'Agriculture, 1875–1985', in G. C. Baugh (ed.), *Victoria History of Shropshire*, vol. IV (Oxford), pp. 232–269.

Robinson, G. M. (1983) *West Midlands Farming 1840s to 1970s: Agricultural Change in the Period between the Corn Laws and the Common Market* (Cambridge). A short but useful regional study covering the counties of Hereford, Shropshire, Staffordshire, Warwickshire and Worcestershire.

Robinson, G. M. (1988) *Agricultural Change: Geographical Studies of British Agriculture* (Edinburgh). An important series of regional and farm product studies from High Farming to the Common Agricultural Policy.

Personal accounts

Gavin, Sir W. (1967) *Ninety Years of Family Farming: The Story of Lord Rayleigh's and Strutt and Parker Farms* (London). An account of one family's successful farming in Essex from the depression of the 1870s onwards.

Haggard, H. R. (1902) *Rural England*, 2 vols (London). This author tends to stress the depressed state of English farming.

Hall, A. D. (1913) *A Pilgrimage of British Farming 1910–1912* (London). A record of journeys over the whole of the British Isles by a correspondent of *The Times*.

Keith, J. (1954) *Fifty Years of Farming* (London). The author ran a large scale (and profitable) farming enterprise in Aberdeenshire and Norfolk from 1903 until his death in 1953.

Mackie, Sir M. (1992) *A Lucky Chap: Orra Loon to Lord Lieutenant* (Buchan). Reminiscences of a successful dairy farmer in north-east Scotland.

Pratt, E. A. (1906) *The Transition in Agriculture* (London). A survey of commercial options available to and adopted by farmers following the decline in cereals, strongly in favour of smallholdings and cooperation.

Street, A. G. (1932) *Farmer's Glory*. Vivid portrait of farming in Wiltshire just before the First World War, during the wartime and post-war boom, and in the depression after the 1921 repeal of the Corn Production Act.

Addendum

Barnes, Pamela (1993) *Norfolk Landowners since 1880* (Norwich, University of East Anglia).

Index

Acts of Parliament: Abnormal
    Importation Act 1931, 55;
    Agricultural Holdings Act 1875
    and 1883, 24; Agricultural
    Marketing Act 1931 and 1932,
    57; Agricultural Rates Act 1901,
    25; Agricultural Rates Acts 1923
    and 1929, 52; Agricultural
    Wages (Regulation) Act 1924,
    44; Agriculture Act 1920, 38–9;
    British (Sugar) Subsidy Act
    1925, 53; Corn Production Act
    1917, 32–4, 38–9; Corn
    Production (Repeal) Act 1921,
    43, 52; Development Fund Act
    1909, 28; Fertilizers and
    Feeding Stuffs Act 1893, 25;
    Gangs Act 1867, 3;
    Horticultural Products
    (Emergency Duties) Act 1931,
    55; Import Duties Act 1932, 55;
    Improvement of Land Act 1899,
    25; Land Settlement (Facilities)
    Act, 67; Market Gardens
    Compensation Act 1895, 25;
    Settled Land Act 1882 and
    1884, 24; Smallholdings and
    Allotments Act 1892, 66; Small
    Holdings Act 1892, 66;
    Technical Instruction Act 1889,
    28; Wheat Act 1932, 58
Agnew of Lochaw 18
Agricultural Wages Board 33–4, 39,
    43
Ailesbury, Marquess of 19
arable farming 14, 21, 43–4, 49
Arch, J. 22
Argentina 8, 38, 54, 56
artificial fertilizers 1–2
Australia 2, 7, 28, 37, 38, 56

bacon factories 59
bankruptcies 19–20, 42
barley 9–10, 26, 32, 34, 38, 46, 57,
    58
Bedford, Duke of 19
Bedfordshire 14
beef 3, 9, 13, 56, 57, 70
Berkshire 6, 19
Beveridge, Sir W. 53, 55
Board of Agriculture 25, 28, 31, 32
*British Farming in the Great Depression
    1870–1914* 15–16
butter: home-produced, 3, 43, 49,
    57, 60, 63, 65, 70; imports 7, 13,
    27, 42, 65, 70

Caird, J. 6, 14
Canada 8, 22–3, 28, 38, 54, 56
capital, *see* investment
cereals, *see* farms, imports, prices,
    output
cheese: factories, 59, 63; farmhouse,
    32, 49, 59, 63, 65, 70; imports,
    23, 27, 42, 60, 70; prices 3, 13,
    43, 57, 60
Cheshire 19–20, 63
consumption: wheat, 10, 27, 47, 58;
    meat 27, 47
co-operatives, *see* farmers
Corn Laws 2
costs 10, 12–13, 23, 27, 31–3, 41,
    43–4, 46, 48, 68
County War Agricultural Executive
    Committees 37

dairy companies 13, 58
dairy farming 13, 15, 18, 21, 29–30,
    46, 49–50, 60
demand for: cereals, 2, 33, 37, 54–5,
    68, 69; labour, 3, 23; land, 40–1;

livestock products 2, 13, 33, 47, 53, 54–5, 70
Denmark 28, 56, 59
Derbyshire 59
Devon 21–2, 28, 63
Disraeli, B. 7
Dorset 59

education 3, 25, 28, 48
emigration 22–3
Empire, *see* imperial preference
England: regions 4–5, 19–20, 23–4, 58–9, 69
English Farming Past & Present 11
Ernle, Lord 11, 15, 19
Essex 18–19, 21, 37, 46, 50
Europe 3, 8, 13, 15, 24, 26, 29, 35, 37, 46, 49, 53, 55, 59, 66

farm investment: current, 50; fixed, 4, 29, 50; landlords', 3–4, 5–6, 19, 30; farmers' 3–4, 49, 50
farm size 12, 14–15, 20, 29, 43–4, 49, 54, 59, 62, 65–7
farmers: co-operatives, 40, 59–60; owner-occupiers, 17, 25, 32, 40, 45, 49; tenants 3, 4–5, 11, 17–21, 24–5, 29–30, 32, 40–1, 45, 67
farmworkers: declining numbers, 17, 22, 24, 65; productivity, 24, 64; training, 29; wages 10, 17, 22–3, 32–4, 38, 40, 43–4, 46, 48, 54, 62
fatstock 41, 43
foreign competition 5, 6, 13, 33, 41, 63
France 2, 26–7
fruit growing 14–15, 25

Galloway, Earl of 18
Germany 35
Girdlestone, Canon 22
grassland 23, 31, 34, 38
'Great Betrayal' 39
Guy's Hospital 18

heavy land 10, 18, 45–7, 50
high farming 1–6, 14, 29–30, 70
horticulture 14
Huntingdon 24, 50

imperial preference 28, 53, 55–7, 61
imports: cereals, 2, 7, 13, 27, 61; fruit, 7, 43, 55–6; dairy products, 7, 55–6; livestock, 3, 8, 27; meat 3, 7–8, 13, 27, 42, 55–6, 60
India 8, 38, 53, 56

Knight, Sir F. 19

landlords 3–4, 17–21, 29–30, 40; allowances 4, 19, 21, 24, 33, 45; land sales 36, 41, *see also* farm investment
Leicester, Earl of 15
Leicestershire 59, 63
light land 4, 10, 45
livestock, *see* farms, imports, prices, output
London 2, 9, 13, 15, 21, 28
London Gazette 9, 19

machinery 3, 23, 44, 48–9, 62–3, 65
market gardens 15, 25, 43, 45, 49, 69, 70
market towns 63
markets: British, 3, 5, 13, 31, 39, 55, 58, 62; world 7, 27, 41, 46
milk: Marketing Boards, 4, 58–9; production 10, 13, 21, 32, 34–5, 43, 48–50, 57–60, 65, 70
Milner Committee 31–2
mixed farming 1, 5, 14–15, 21, 48–9, 70
Murray-Stewart of Broughton 18
mutton: home produced, 9, 13, 18, 70; imports 13, 56

National Farmers' Union 38, 40
New Zealand 7, 22, 28, 56
Norfolk 2, 15, 42, 44, 53

oats 9–10, 26, 32–4, 38–40, 57–8
Ottawa Conference 55–7
output: cereal, 3, 10, 31–2, 35; livestock 1–2, 5, 9–15, 19–21, 24, 29, 33–5, 37, 45–8, 50, 62, 68–70
overseas investment 46, 47

prices: animal products, 3, 9–10, 12,

14–15, 18, 20, 27, 29–30, 35, 43, 47, 51, 58–60; cereals, 3, 7, 9, 10, 12, 14, 23, 26, 33, 34, 38–9, 43–4, 46, 50, 53, 68; general, 16, 33, 37, 40–3, 45–7, 49–60, 68–70; guaranteed 31–3, 38–40, 58
profits 14, 24, 33, 40, 41, 43, 45, 47–8, 67–8

Rayleigh, Lord 21
rents 4–5, 13, 15, 17–19, 21, 32, 36, 45, 52, 67
Robbins, L. 53
Royal Commissions on Agricultural Depression 11–12
rural trades and industries 63–4
Russia 2, 7–8, 28

seasons 3, 7, 10
Scotland 1–2, 4–5, 11, 13, 18, 22–3, 34, 39, 44, 48, 51, 53, 59
smallholdings 65–6
Stanier, Sir B. 45
store animals 5, 41, 51
Strutt, E. 21
subsidies 53, 57–8, 60
sugar beet 5, 41, 51–3
sugar beet factories 52–3
Sutherland, Duke of 18–19

Tariffs: The Case Examined 53–5

tariff protection 25–7, 29–30, 46, 52–8
taxes: central, 28, 36, 39, 53, 60, 67; local 25, 52, 60, 67
tenant compensation 4, 21, 25, 39
towns 2, 40, 62–3, 66
trade unions 22
transport: domestic, 2, 13–14, 24, 60, 63, 70; international 7

underdrainage 3, 24, 47, 50, 64
United States 2, 7–8, 56

vegetables 10, 14–15, 21, 26, 43, 46–7, 50, 55–6, 70

wages, *see* Agricultural Wages Board, farmworkers
Wales 5, 11, 18–22, 24, 31, 34, 39, 42, 44–5, 48–9, 51–2, 58–60, 64, 69–70
wars: American Civil, 27; Boer, 27; Crimean, 2; First World, 16, 23, 31–6; Franco-Prussian, 2; Napoleonic, 25; Russo-Turkish 7
Westminster, Duke of 19
wheat, 3, 7–10, 12, 14, 18, 23, 25–7, 29–30, 32, 34–5, 37–42, 46–9, 50, 53–8, 60, 69; *see also* consumption
Wiltshire 13, 19, 63
Women's Land Army 34
Worcester 59

New Studies in Economic and Social History

Titles in the series available from Cambridge University Press:

1. M. Anderson
   Approaches to the history of the Western family, 1500–1914

2. W. Macpherson
   The economic development of Japan, 1868–1941

3. R. Porter
   Disease, medicine, and society in England: second edition

4. B.W.E. Alford
   British economic performance since 1945

5. A. Crowther
   Social policy in Britain, 1914–1939

6. E. Roberts
   Women's work 1840–1940

7. C. O'Grada
   The great Irish famine

8. R. Rodger
   Housing in urban Britain 1780–1914

9. P. Slack
   The English Poor Law 1531–1782

10. J.L. Anderson
    Explaining long-term economic change

11. D. Baines
    Emigration from Europe 1815–1930

12. M. Collins
    Banks and industrial finance 1800–1939

13. A. Dyer
    Decline and growth in English towns 1400–1640

14. R.B. Outhwaite
    Dearth, public policy and social disturbance in England, 1550–1800

15. M. Sanderson
    Education, economic change and society in England

16. R.D. Anderson
    Universities and elites in Britain since 1800

17. C. Heywood
    The development of the French economy, 1700–1914

18. R.A. Houston
    The population history of Britain and Ireland 1500–1750

19. A.J. Reid
    Social classes and social relations in Britain 1850–1914

20. R. Woods
    The population of Britain in the nineteenth century

21. T.C. Barker
    The rise and rise of road transport, 1700–1990

22. J. Harrison
    The Spanish economy

23. C. Schmitz
    The growth of big business in the United States and Western Europe, 1850–1939

24. R.A. Church
    The rise and decline of the British motor industry

25. P. Horn
    Children's work and welfare, 1780–1880

26. R. Perren
    Agriculture in depression, 1870–1940

27. R.J. Overy
    The Nazi economic recovery 1932–1938: second edition

Previously published as

Studies in Economic History

Titles in the series available from the Macmillan Press Limited

1. B.W.E. Alford
   Depression and recovery? British economic growth, 1918–1939

2. M. Anderson
   Population change in north-western Europe, 1750–1850

3. S.D. Chapman
   The cotton industry in the industrial revolution: second edition

4. N. Charlesworth
   British rule and the Indian economy, 1800–1914

5. L.A. Clarkson
   Proto-industrialisation: the first phase of industrialisation

6. D.C. Coleman
   Industry in Tudor and Stuart England

7. I.M. Drummond
   The gold standard and the international monetary system, 1900–1939

8. M.E. Falkus
   The industrialisation of Russia, 1700–1914

9. J.R. Harris
   The British iron industry, 1700–1850

10. J. Hatcher
    Plague, population and the English economy, 1348–1530

11. J.R. Hay
    The origins of the Liberal welfare reforms, 1906–1914

12. H. McLeod
    Religion and the working classes in nineteenth-century Britain

13. J.D. Marshall
    The Old Poor Law 1795–1834: second edition

14. R.J. Morris
    Class and class consciousness in the industrial revolution, 1750–1850

15. P.K. O'Brien
    The economic effects of the American civil war

16. P.L. Payne
    British entrepreneurship in the nineteenth century

17. G.C. Peden
    Keynes, the treasury and British economic policy

18. M.E. Rose
    The relief of poverty, 1834–1914

19. J. Thirsk
    England's agricultural regions and agrarian history, 1500–1750

20. J.R. Ward
    Poverty and progress in the Caribbean, 1800–1960

Economic History Society

The Economic History Society, which numbers around 3,000 members, publishes the *Economic History Review* four times a year (free to members) and holds an annual conference.

Enquiries about membership should be addressed to

The Assistant Secretary
Economic History Society
PO Box 70
Kingswood
Bristol
BS15 5TB

Full-time students may join at special rates.